EAT

with

BEDER

RECIPES AND REFLECTIONS FROM WELL KNOWN PERSONALITIES
AND INSPIRATIONAL INDIVIDUALS RAISING AWARENESS AROUND
MENTAL HEALTH AND SUICIDE PREVENTION

EAT *with* BEDER

First edition printed in 2022 in the UK
ISBN: 978-1-910863-95-4
Written by: Razzak Mirjan
Photography by: Kimberley Espinel
Edited by: Katie Fisher, Phil Turner
Designed by: Paul Cocker
Sales & PR: Emma Toogood, Lizzy Capps
Contributors: Lis Ellis, Megan Georgia,
Lizzie Morton

Printed in Great Britain
by Bell and Bain Ltd, Glasgow

Published by Meze Publishing Limited
Unit 1b, 2 Kelham Square
Kelham Riverside
Sheffield S3 8SD
Web: www.mezepublishing.co.uk
Telephone: 0114 275 7709
Email: info@mezepublishing.co.uk

Beder is a registered charity in England and Wales (No. 1187475).

INTRODUCTION

Welcome to Eat with Beder, our second and most special cookbook yet.

Eat with Beder showcases the power of food to bring people together. With the help of many amazing contributors, we have created a cookbook filled with recipes for every occasion which I cannot wait for you and those joining you around the table to enjoy!

We have all been through some truly testing times over the last few years, but the pandemic has also helped us understand the importance of togetherness, power of community, need for self-care and necessity of looking after our mental health.

As a charity, Beder aims to bring people together who share similar interests and provide a platform for us all to play our part in raising awareness around mental health and suicide. Through these interests, we are able to softly raise awareness and build a community of like-minded people.

Eat with Beder has been created with these pillars at its heart.

We have gathered an array of incredible individuals from diverse professions and backgrounds who have come together through their desire to support Beder in its work to overcome the stigma surrounding mental health and suicide.

Each recipe has been developed by leading recipe writers to bring each individual's personality and culinary tastes to life in the essence of a recipe. You will find simple yet delicious breakfasts, quick weekday meals, wholesome dishes and mouth-watering desserts which you'll want to make again and again.

Eat with Beder is also filled with honest and insightful reflections, from personal experiences to words of advice, generously shared by the contributors. We hope to encourage people to understand that prioritising your mental health is not something to be ashamed of and talking about what is on your mind can often help you realise there are others that have been through similar times. Everyone can struggle with their mental health, so let's be kind to ourselves and others.

Thank you from the bottom of my heart to everyone who has helped bring Eat with Beder to life, as it was a huge team effort. I would also like to thank you for purchasing a copy because in doing so you are enabling us to make a significant difference, as a charity and as a family, to continue to do good in my brother's memory.

I hope your time in the kitchen is always enjoyable and that this cookbook helps to create some wonderful memories, so put on your apron, gather your friends and family and let's Eat with Beder.

Yours,

Razzak Mirjan

ABOUT EAT WITH BEDER

Eat with Beder is a charity cookbook containing a unique collection of recipes and reflections from well known personalities and inspirational individuals including Steven Bartlett, Joanna Lumley, Theo Paphitis, Giovanna Fletcher, Dame Kelly Holmes, Ella Mills, Stuart Broad and many more to raise awareness around mental health and suicide prevention in support of Beder.

Each recipe has been created especially for the contributor to reflect their tastes and personality by leading recipe writers which ensures that Eat with Beder contains a diverse array of exciting recipes for you to enjoy.

Each chapter has a different theme: Start Your Day The Right Way contains delicious recipes for breakfast and brunch; Happy Gut, Happy Life is filled with nutritious and healthy recipes; Fast Food (but not as you know it!) provides mouth-watering recipes which can be made if you are short of time; Soul Food is packed with everyone's favourite dishes; and Sweet Treats offers scrumptious desserts and baking recipes.

Eat with Beder contains honest and inspiring conversations around the table with some of the cookbook's contributors as they talk openly about their own journey and experiences with mental health, offering readers a chance to get to know the individual behind the personality.

For many people, cooking or baking is a form of therapy, and research supports the fact that cooking is good for your mental health as it provides an outlet for creative expression, a means for communication and can be an act of mindfulness. Of course, there are other ways to look after our mental health but creating good food at home is a great place to start.

We hope you enjoy reading, learning and cooking from Eat with Beder as much as we have enjoyed bringing this very special project together.

> Eat with Beder contains honest and inspiring conversations around the table with some of the cookbook's contributors as they talk openly about their own journey and experiences with mental health, offering readers a chance to get to know the individual behind the personality.

ABOUT BEDER

Beder is a charity taking a unique approach to softly raising awareness around mental health and suicide prevention.

Beder was founded in memory of Beder Mirjan by his older brother, Razzak Mirjan, in November 2019.

As a family, we took the collective decision to start a charity in Beder's name because while it is not possible to rewrite history and have him with us today, we believe there are positives that can be found from our darkest days.

Our aim is to lead the way collaboratively, building meaningful relationships with our supporters whilst creating greater accessibility to information and opportunities that help everyone to manage their mental health and make time for self-care.

We are working hard to challenge the stigma surrounding mental health and suicide prevention and to provide a platform for us all to play our part in normalising the conversation around these important societal issues.

Beder has partnered with Shout, a leading mental health charity, and Samaritans, an established and highly respected charity working across the UK and Ireland focused on reducing suicide. The aims of these partnerships are to harness the specialist knowledge of Shout and Samaritans, as well as promote and further both charities' incredible work.

Since founding Beder, we have organised a range of in-person events and initiatives including mindful painting sessions, sports events, cooking classes and music concerts at venues such as Union Chapel and The Jazz Cafe in London in addition to fitness, meditation and yoga classes.

We published our first cookbook, From Beder's Kitchen, in November 2020 which brought together a range of amazing foodies from all over the world and has been sold internationally. We also created a Christmas advent calendar filled with physical and digital products focused on looking after your mental health and encouraging self-care.

As we adjust to the new normal following the pandemic, everyone is realising the importance of connection and community.

The Beder community continues to grow quickly, as these are issues that affect a significant number of people on a daily basis, so if you would like to find out more or get involved with Beder, we would love to hear from you!

Whether you're interested in fundraising for Beder, representing the charity in a mass participation event, hosting an event in support of us, or simply having a chat, please do contact us for more information.

To donate or find out more about Beder, please visit our website at www.beder.org.uk or email us at inspire@beder.org.uk.

BEDER MIRJAN

Beder Mirjan was a giant of a young man, with a witty sense of humour and an infectious laugh, who was gentle, caring, polite and kind natured.

He was incredibly intelligent, hard working and in love with anything related to aircraft, flying, computers and watches, among other things.

Beder was always surrounded by love and due to start university with a bright future ahead of him. However, he made the unexpected decision to take his own life at the age of 18 in April 2017.

We will never know the exact reasons for his decision, which makes coming to terms with his choice incredibly hard to process for those fortunate enough to have crossed paths with him, but we hope that Beder is now in peace and free from the dark thoughts that clouded his mind.

This is not how it was supposed to be, but, through Beder as a charity, we are working our hardest to normalise the conversation around mental health and suicide.

Our goal is to help people realise that it is okay not to be okay, and showing vulnerability or asking for help is not a sign of weakness. You are not alone, and those feelings that seem like something no one else will understand are feelings that so many others experience as well. Suicide is not inevitable; it is preventable.

It is important to never take those around us for granted and cherish even the simplest moments, as we never know what the future holds. It can be difficult to talk about someone who has taken their own life, or know what to say when someone brings their name up in conversation. That's understandable, but as we continue to mention their name or talk about the good times that we shared, we also give others the strength to share what's on their mind.

Our charity, Beder, and this cookbook are in memory of Beder Mirjan.

> It can be difficult to talk about someone who has taken their own life, or know what to say when someone brings their name up in conversation. That's understandable, but as we continue to mention their name or talk about the good times that we shared, we also give others the strength to share what's on their mind.

THANK YOU FROM BEDER

We are unbelievably grateful to everyone who has supported this project and helped bring Eat with Beder to life!

Our thank you list is lengthy but incredibly important and, in no particular order, includes:

Each contributor that has taken the time to support Beder and engaged with our unique approach to softly raising awareness around mental health and suicide prevention. We have loved creating your recipes for this special cookbook and we hope you enjoy them!

Our recipe writers, namely **Liberty Mendez**, **Lily Gjertsen**, **Safia Shakarchi**, **Anna Lawson**, **Susan Morrison** and **Elena Silcock** as this cookbook would not exist without your hard work, creativity and commitment.

Our incredible suppliers for their remarkable generosity including:

County Supplies, with special thanks to **Elizabeth Hurren** and **Liam Kelly**, for providing plentiful supplies of the freshest fruit, vegetables and herbs once again. Find out more at: www.countysupplies.com.

Fin & Bone, with special thanks to **Alex Taylor** and the team, for supplying top quality fish and shellfish. Find out more at: www.finandbone.co.uk or visit this amazing butcher and fishmonger at 303 New King's Road, London, SW6 4RF.

Waitrose, with special thanks to **Tor Alcock** and **Lisa Wyatt**, for supplying a wide range of ingredients and meat.

Our publishers, **Meze Publishing**, with special thanks to **Phil Turner**, **Katie Fisher**, **Paul Cocker**, **Emma Toogood** and **Lizzy Capps** for your hard work to bring everything together ahead of schedule. It has been a pleasure working with you again.

Kimberly Espinel, as our photographer, for bringing an amazing energy, passion and calmness from the moment you joined the Eat with Beder team. Your work is excellent and it was a lot of fun to work with you.

Katie Marshall, as our food stylist, for your creativity, composure, hard work and flexibility during very busy and demanding days on set whilst remaining in high spirits throughout. You were amazing and an invaluable member of the team.

Megan Thomson, as our prop stylist, for selecting excellent props for each recipe and diligently staying on top of everything whilst at the photoshoot. It was also great to have you involved as our veteran member of the team having assisted previously on From Beder's Kitchen.

Our food styling assistants, namely **Lucy Joseph**, **Jenny Craig**, **Sophie Edwards** and **Valerie Russo** for their energy, hard work and enthusiasm, in addition to our photography assistants, for their support and assistance.

Clear Channel, with special thanks to **Glyn Palmer** and **Nick Andrews**, for putting Eat with Beder on billboards nationwide and helping spread the word in ways which we simply couldn't have imagined.

Plus Agency, with special thanks to **Chris West** and **Tom Lardner**, for generously agreeing to create eye-catching artwork and provide all of the assets which we needed to maximise our nationwide out-of-home campaign.

The Beder team, with special thanks to **Chloe Hodgkinson** and **Harry Parker** for your continued flexibility and commitment to Beder, in addition to our **trustees** and **ambassadors**.

Finally, **our supporters and partners** for your invaluable support and belief in our approach, events and initiatives to raising awareness around these important issues.

We are unbelievably grateful to everyone who has supported
this project and helped bring Eat with Beder to life!

CONTENTS

CHAPTER 3 - FAST FOOD (BUT NOT AS YOU KNOW IT)

CHAPTER 4 - SOUL FOOD

CHAPTER 5 - SWEET TREATS

CHAPTER

1

START YOUR DAY THE RIGHT WAY

This chapter features an array of breakfast and brunch recipes worth getting out of bed for, inspired by cuisines around the world.

HONEY & SESAME MUESLI BARS

PREPARATION TIME: 5-20 MINUTES, PLUS CHILLING | COOKING TIME: 5 MINUTES | MAKES 8

INGREDIENTS

150g unsalted butter, cubed

60g tahini

50g dark brown sugar

30g honey

Pinch of flaky sea salt

200g rolled porridge oats

50g sesame seeds (black or white)

50g mixed seeds (we used pumpkin and sunflower)

50g mixed nuts, roughly chopped

75g dried fruit (we used cranberries and apricots)

METHOD

Line a 25cm by 20cm tin with non-stick greaseproof paper.

Put the butter, tahini, sugar, honey and salt into a saucepan over a medium heat.

Stir until everything has melted together, then set aside.

In a large frying pan over a medium heat, toast the oats, sesame seeds, mixed seeds and nuts for 3-4 minutes, stirring constantly, until everything is starting to turn golden and smell toasty.

Pour the toasted oat mixture and dried fruit into the melted butter mixture, then stir to combine until all the dry ingredients are coated.

Press the mixture into the lined tin and flatten down with the back of a spoon (wet the spoon if it's sticking) until the top is flat and the mixture is evenly distributed.

Cover and put in the fridge for 3 hours or overnight until set.

Once set, remove from the tin and use a sharp knife to cut into 8 rectangles.

Spending as much time with my friends as I can helps me look after my mental health. I also find preparing ingredients, such as peeling and chopping, helps me relax. If I could talk to my younger self, I would remind them that mental health is very real and needs attention just like your physical health.

WILL GREENWOOD (@WILLGREENWOOD)

TURKISH EGGS WITH FETA & CHILLI BUTTER

PREPARATION TIME: 5-20 MINUTES | COOKING TIME: 10 MINUTES | SERVES 2

INGREDIENTS

225g Greek yoghurt

60g feta, crumbled

½ clove of garlic, grated

½ lemon, juiced

Flaky sea salt

50g unsalted butter

½ tsp Turkish chilli flakes, plus extra to serve

4 eggs

60ml white vinegar

TO SERVE

A few sprigs of soft herbs, chopped (such as dill or coriander)

Sourdough or flatbread

METHOD

In a bowl, combine the Greek yoghurt with half the feta and the grated garlic, lemon juice and a good pinch of flaky sea salt.

Whisk well until smooth, breaking up the feta as you go.

Melt the butter in a small saucepan over a gentle heat. You can leave it to sizzle and brown slightly for a nuttier flavour but watch it carefully as it can quickly burn.

Remove from the heat, add the chilli flakes and set aside.

Crack the eggs into small ramekins and bring a medium saucepan of water to the boil.

Once boiling, add the vinegar. Using a spoon, create a whirlpool in the boiling water and gently pour the eggs into the centre of the whirlpool one after the other. Depending on the size of your pan you may need to poach the eggs 2 at a time.

Reduce the heat to a simmer and set a timer for 3 minutes.

Remove the eggs from the pan and drain on a plate lined with kitchen towel.

TO SERVE

Swirl the yoghurt mixture over two plates and pour a little chilli butter over it.

Top with two poached eggs each and divide the remaining chilli butter over the top.

Finish with the remaining feta, fresh herbs and a sprinkle of chilli flakes, if you like.

Serve with some toasted sourdough or warmed flatbread to mop it all up.

> I love cooking and it certainly takes my mind off things. Other things I do to look after my mental health include waking up early, exercising and always doing something that brings a big smile to my face each day. I also think it's important not to judge my happiness based purely on my work.
>
> STUART BROAD (@STUARTBROAD)

PEAR & TAHINI PORRIDGE

PREPARATION TIME: 5-20 MINUTES | COOKING TIME: 5 MINUTES | SERVES 2

INGREDIENTS

1 ½ tbsp tahini

½ tsp vanilla extract

1 soft pear

55g porridge oats

350ml cashew milk

1 tsp maple syrup

METHOD

Mix the tahini and vanilla extract together in a small bowl.

Cut the pear in half lengthways, then dice one half and cut the other half into long spears.

Place the oats, diced pear, cashew milk and maple syrup into a pan over a medium heat and simmer for 4-5 minutes.

Divide the porridge between 2 bowls and fan the pear spears out on each one.

TO SERVE

Drizzle the vanilla tahini mixture over the top.

It's important to talk about mental health as many, myself included in the past, suffer in silence. I try to be open and aware of what I am feeling and going through, so I can attempt to figure things out from a point of awareness.

DALE PINNOCK (@THEMEDICINALCHEF)

THERE ARE SO MANY PRESSURES
TO ACT AND FEEL A CERTAIN WAY
WHEN, IN REALITY, THERE IS
NO GREATER DISPLAY OF STRENGTH
THAN ALLOWING YOURSELF TO FEEL
COMFORTABLE WITH WHO YOU ARE.

BEN WEST

ACV LEMON TONIC

PREPARATION TIME: 5 MINUTES | SERVES 1

INGREDIENTS

1 cup of green tea, chilled

1 tbsp apple cider vinegar

2 tsp grated fresh ginger

1 tsp honey

1 lemon

METHOD

Boil a kettle and make a cup of green tea.

Allow the green tea to cool then chill in the fridge.

Stir the chilled tea, apple cider vinegar, grated ginger and honey together in a glass.

Add a squeeze of lemon juice to taste and enjoy!

> Mental health is incredibly important to me, and something that affects us all. Since starting Willy's ACV, I've learnt so much about the connection between the mind and the gut and how this is so critical to overall health and wellbeing. It turns out you really are what you eat! I love to experiment in the kitchen with healthy, live, fermented foods as part of looking after my own mental health.
>
> WILLIAM CHASE

SEEDED SODA BREAD

PREPARATION TIME: 10-25 MINUTES | COOKING TIME: 40 MINUTES | MAKES 1 LOAF

INGREDIENTS

1 lemon, juiced

315-375ml whole milk

225g plain flour

225g wholemeal flour (or spelt wholemeal)

1 tsp bicarbonate of soda

1 tsp fine salt

1 tsp sugar

40g mixed seeds

METHOD

Preheat the oven to 200°c/180°c fan/Gas Mark 6.

Pour the lemon juice into the milk and set aside for 2 minutes. This will curdle slightly and act as buttermilk. If you can find real buttermilk, you can use that instead.

Pour the plain flour, wholemeal flour, bicarbonate of soda, salt and sugar into a mixing bowl and stir to combine.

Gradually add the curdled milk to the dry ingredients – you may not need it all. Mix with your hands until you reach a soft but not sticky consistency.

Once the mixture has come together, knead for 2 minutes to get a smooth dough and then shape into a ball.

Place this on a non-stick baking tray and brush some water all over the dough.

Press the seeds gently into the dough so they stick all the way across the top of the ball.

Using a sharp knife, score a cross on top of the loaf, dragging your knife in one direction for a clean line.

Bake the soda bread in the preheated oven for 40 minutes until golden brown.

Leave to cool on a wire rack before slicing and serving with butter and honey or jam.

Positive mental health is so important. It isn't discussed enough and is so fragile for so many because of the pandemic. I believe we always need to prioritise it, especially during the middle years of raising your children and coping with elderly parents. I try to have 'switch off' time with my close family or by doing yoga, Pilates and outdoor running. Although I'm not a natural cook, I love spending my weekends baking or making big one-pot dishes that bring lots of ingredients together.

SHARON WHITE

COURGETTE, LEMON & FETA BREAKFAST FRITTERS

PREPARATION TIME: 15-30 MINUTES | COOKING TIME: 10 MINUTES | SERVES 2

INGREDIENTS

250g courgettes
(approx. 1.5-2 courgettes)

1 tbsp chopped fresh dill

1 tbsp chopped fresh mint

1 tbsp chopped fresh coriander

1 tsp ground cumin

30g flour

1 spring onion, finely sliced

½ lemon, zested

70g feta

3 eggs

30ml white vinegar

Vegetable oil, for frying

Sea salt and black pepper

Greek yoghurt, to serve (optional)

METHOD

Grate the courgettes (with the skin still on) into a j-cloth or cheesecloth.

Wring out as much excess liquid as possible in the sink, then leave the grated courgette to drain in a sieve while you prepare the other ingredients.

Combine the fresh herbs, cumin, flour, spring onion, lemon zest, feta and 1 egg in a large mixing bowl.

Add the drained courgette and mix well, scraping the bottom of the bowl to ensure everything is incorporated. Season with sea salt and black pepper to taste, then shape the mixture into patties about 6cm in diameter.

Heat a thin layer of oil in a frying pan over a medium-high heat.

Fry for 3-4 minutes on each side, or until golden and crisp. You may need to do this in a few batches depending on the size of your pan.

Crack the eggs into small ramekins and bring a medium saucepan of water to the boil.

Once boiling, add the vinegar. Using a spoon, create a whirlpool in the boiling water and gently pour the eggs into the centre of the whirlpool one after the other. Depending on the size of your pan you may need to poach the eggs 2 at a time.

Reduce the heat to a simmer and set a timer for 3 minutes.

Remove the poached eggs from the pan and drain on a plate lined with kitchen towel.

Place 2-3 fritters per person on each plate, topped with a poached egg and a dollop of Greek yoghurt, if you like.

Scatter with fresh herbs and finish with a twist of black pepper.

> There are many things I wish I could tell my younger self! But it's too late now, so I try to focus on what I can do for my future self instead, and I have my own youth mental health charity called Beyond to help the next generation with their mental health. So many young people feel anxious, isolated and now traumatised due to the pandemic. Don't underestimate the power of activities like cooking, which can be the perfect therapeutic opportunity to talk about wellbeing. Give it a try and see what happens!

JONNY BENJAMIN (@MRJONNYBENJAMIN)

SUMAC BAKED FETA WITH CRISPY CHICKPEAS & HARISSA YOGHURT

PREPARATION TIME: 10-25 MINUTES | COOKING TIME: 35 MINUTES | SERVES 2-4

INGREDIENTS

1 large onion, peeled and thinly sliced

2 cloves of garlic, peeled and diced

250g cherry tomatoes, halved

1 x 400g tin of chickpeas, drained

100g pine nuts

2 tsp paprika

1 tsp dried oregano

1 tsp dried rosemary

2 tsp sumac

Sea salt

Olive oil

1 block of feta (about 200g)

FOR THE HARISSA YOGHURT

200g Greek-style yoghurt

2 tbsp rose harissa

1 lemon, juiced

TO SERVE

Handful of chopped parsley

Small handful of pine nuts

METHOD

Preheat the oven to 220°c/200°c fan/Gas Mark 7.

Place the onion, garlic, cherry tomatoes, chickpeas and pine nuts into a large ovenproof baking dish.

Add the paprika, oregano, rosemary, 1 teaspoon of sumac and a pinch of salt.

Mix well until everything is coated in the spices before drizzling in olive oil, then mix again until it's all coated in the oil.

Place the feta on top of the vegetables in the dish. Drizzle it with olive oil and season with the remaining sumac and a pinch of salt.

Cook the whole dish in the preheated oven for 25-30 minutes until the vegetables are cooked through and crispy on the outside.

FOR THE HARISSA YOGHURT

Mix the yoghurt with the harissa, lemon juice and a pinch of salt in a small bowl.

TO SERVE

Once the feta and chickpea mixture has finished baking, transfer the dish from the oven to the table and serve up with some extra parsley and pine nuts sprinkled on top, and the harissa yoghurt on the side.

> Taking care of your inner self is as essential as looking after your physical body. Allow yourself lots of time for rest, relaxation and reflection and when things feel tough, reach out and talk. For me, walking and being outside in fresh air, spending time with loved ones and being open when things feel tough help me to look after my mental health.
>
> JULIE BENTLEY (@JULIEBENTLEY)

STEVEN BARTLETT

REACHING BREAKING POINT

I've seen first-hand the impact that stress, burn-out and anxiety can have on friends and colleagues. When I started Social Chain with one of my best friends, the cost of making millions was excruciatingly severe. We were just two young university dropouts in our early twenties, working every single day, every weekend, glued to our phones 24/7.

Facing high pressure decisions that would ultimately make or break the business will always take a toll on your headspace and mindset. But amongst all of this, we didn't actually speak to each other about how we were feeling. It was only after my business partner Dom reached breaking point and some pretty extreme actions were taken that we were forced into a conversation about how we were really feeling.

LOOKING AFTER OTHERS

Since then, I have been so determined to make day-to-day chats about our mental health normal. We introduced free therapy at Social Chain to ensure everyone always had someone to speak to. I now make a point of asking my friends how they're feeling on a regular basis and asking twice to get the real answer. You never know how much impact a simple check-in text might have on someone's day.

LOOKING AFTER MYSELF

Working out regularly definitely helps my mental health, so I try to do something physical every day. I write a lot down in my diary, as writing helps relieve my mind after a long day. I also talk now, with my girlfriend, my friends and my colleagues. Our thoughts can be so overwhelmingly loud sometimes and the less we keep bottled up, the better in my opinion.

MY ADVICE TO YOU

Based on personal experience, I would advise anyone to stop avoiding conversations with best friends about how we are all feeling. It's so important and I avoided the subject completely when I was younger. Looking after your mental health has a positive effect on everything else you do. Your health in all forms must be your priority.

BOMBAY MASALA OMELETTE

PREPARATION TIME: 10-25 MINUTES | COOKING TIME: 5 MINUTES | SERVES 1

INGREDIENTS

2 large eggs

2 spring onions, thinly sliced

1 medium vine tomato, diced

½ red chilli, finely chopped

Handful of fresh coriander, roughly chopped (plus extra to serve)

¼ tsp garam masala

¼ tsp cumin

Salt and pepper

Knob of butter

METHOD

Crack the eggs into a bowl and whisk.

Add the spring onions, tomato, chilli, coriander and spices.

Mix again to make sure everything is well combined and distributed, then season to taste.

Heat the butter in a frying pan over a medium heat and pour in the egg mixture.

Swirl the pan to cover the base with the mixture and leave to cook for a few minutes. Once the mixture is just set, fold the omelette in half and transfer to a plate.

Serve with fresh coriander and sliced red chilli on top, if you like.

"

It's not so much the practice of cooking itself that helps my mental health; sitting down and enjoying food with friends and family is what I really love. Getting friends and family together and eating around the table is always where great discussions happen, and you can truly connect with people.

STEVEN BARTLETT (@STEVEN)

CRISPY POTATO LATKES WITH SOUR CREAM, SMOKED SALMON & POACHED EGGS

PREPARATION TIME: 15-30 MINUTES | COOKING TIME: 10 MINUTES | SERVES 2

INGREDIENTS

300g starchy potatoes (Maris Piper or King Edward work well)

1 medium onion

40g plain flour

1 large egg

Vegetable oil, for frying

2 eggs

30ml white vinegar

100g sour cream

A few slices of smoked salmon

1 spring onion, thinly sliced

Fresh dill, roughly chopped

METHOD

Coarsely grate the potatoes (with the skin still on) and the onion into a j-cloth or cheesecloth lining a large bowl.

Bring the corners of the cloth together and wring out as much excess liquid from the mixture as possible over the sink.

Mix the drained potato and onion with the flour and egg in a bowl, then season to taste.

Heat a frying pan over a medium heat and cover with an even layer of oil.

Create 6 small, thin patties with the potato mixture using your hands and gently fry for 1½-2 minutes on each side, or until golden brown and crisp. You may need to do this in batches depending on the size of your pan.

Crack the eggs into small ramekins and bring a medium saucepan of water to the boil.

Once boiling, add the vinegar. Using a spoon, create a whirlpool in the boiling water and gently pour the eggs into the centre of the whirlpool one after the other. Depending on the size of your pan you may need to poach the eggs 2 at a time.

Reduce the heat to a simmer and set a timer for 3 minutes.

Remove the poached eggs from the pan and drain on a plate lined with kitchen towel.

Put 2-3 latkes per person on each plate with a dollop of sour cream, a slice or two of smoked salmon, a poached egg, some sliced spring onion and fresh dill on top.

> I know how my mind works and what my triggers are, so I do what I can when I can to take control. Exercise always helps to balance my mind and ease anxiety. I love being outside, walking and absorbing the nature around me as it helps to calm me down and keep me focused. Music also really helps me to feel good. I find talking things over with people is vital to release your thoughts, share how you feel and remember that it's perfectly normal to struggle at times.

CHARLIE KING (@CHARLIE_KING85)

CHOCOLATE CHUNK BANANA PANCAKES WITH HAZELNUTS & MAPLE SYRUP

PREPARATION TIME: 10-25 MINUTES | COOKING TIME: 10 MINUTES | SERVES 2-3

INGREDIENTS

180g self-raising flour

½ tsp baking powder

Pinch of sea salt

1 very ripe banana, mashed

1 large egg

120ml whole milk

50g dark chocolate, roughly chopped

Knob of butter

TO SERVE

1 ripe banana, sliced

50g hazelnuts, toasted and chopped

Maple syrup, to taste

Dark chocolate, roughly chopped

METHOD

Combine the flour, baking powder and salt in a mixing bowl.

In a jug, whisk the mashed banana, egg and milk together.

Make a well in the dry ingredients and pour in the liquid, gently whisking together to create a smooth batter.

Add the roughly chopped chocolate and mix again until evenly combined.

Melt the knob of butter in a frying pan over a gentle heat.

Add a few tablespoons of batter per pancake and cook for about 1 minute 30 seconds or until golden brown, before flipping onto the other side and cooking for the same amount of time.

Repeat with the remaining batter while keeping the cooked pancakes warm.

TO SERVE

Plate up a stack of 3-4 pancakes per person and top with slices of fresh banana, a scattering of chopped toasted hazelnuts, a drizzle of maple syrup and some extra chopped chocolate, if you like.

> Your mental health isn't something to feel embarrassed about. It isn't a weakness. It's learning about who you are and what makes you work. My struggles have taught me more about myself than I could ever imagine. My only regret is not being able to talk about it earlier. I take time for myself now, even if it's just an hour – it's amazing what a walk alone with some music can do. Realising how important food is to your health has been vital as well, and I don't just mean eating vegetables… the naughty food can be just as useful!
>
> JAMES GILLESPIE (@JGILLESPIEINSTA)

LISTEN TO YOURSELF,
LISTEN TO YOUR BODY.
STOP WHEN YOU NEED TO.
YOU KNOW YOURSELF
BETTER THAN ANYONE ELSE.

NADIYA HUSSAIN

CACAO, PEANUT BUTTER &
BANANA BREAKFAST SMOOTHIE

PREPARATION TIME: 5 MINUTES | SERVES 1

INGREDIENTS

220ml almond milk

1-2 tbsp peanut butter

1 large very ripe banana

1 tsp cacao powder

Handful of ice cubes

Pinch of sea salt

Honey, to taste

1 tsp cacao nibs

METHOD

Place all the ingredients except the cacao nibs into a blender and whizz at a high speed until smooth.

Add the cacao nibs and whizz once more just briefly; you want them to grind down a little but still be crunchy.

Pour the smoothie into a large glass, sprinkle with a few more cacao nibs and enjoy!

"

I believe that what you put into your body plays a massive part in how you feel. I know if I'm cooking and eating properly, I feel good, and I love to follow a daily routine which involves lots of exercise.

TOMMY BRADY (@TOMMYBRADY7)

HOMEMADE SESAME BAGELS

PREPARATION TIME: 30-45 MINUTES, PLUS PROVING | COOKING TIME: 30 MINUTES | MAKES 8

INGREDIENTS

500g strong white flour, plus extra for dusting

35g white toasted sesame seeds

35g black sesame seeds

7g fast action dried yeast

3 tbsp caster sugar

1½ tsp fine sea salt

Olive oil, to grease

Flaky sea salt

1 egg, beaten (or 2-3 tbsp dairy-free milk)

METHOD

Put the strong white flour into a mixing bowl with 25g of white and black sesame seeds.

Add the yeast and sugar to one side of the bowl and the salt to the other.

Mix the dry ingredients together, then gradually pour in 300-325ml of lukewarm water and stir to combine. Using just enough to make a soft, slightly sticky dough.

Place the dough onto a clean surface lightly dusted with flour and knead for 10 minutes until you have a smooth ball. Alternatively, use a stand mixer with a dough hook.

Lightly grease a large bowl with olive oil, then put the ball of dough into it and cover with a damp tea towel, leaving to prove for 1 hour, until doubled in size.

Place your risen dough onto a lightly floured surface and divide into 8 equal pieces (around 112g each). Shape each piece into a ball by folding the sides of the dough up and into themselves, then placing each piece seam side down on the work surface.

Place them, spread slightly apart, on a lightly floured tray, cover with a damp tea towel and leave to rest for 10 minutes.

Preheat the oven to 220°c/200°c fan/Gas Mark 7.

Meanwhile, mix the remaining sesame seeds with a pinch of sea salt for the topping.

Once your dough balls have rested, place your thumb and index finger into the centre of each ball and move it around to make a hole about 3cm wide.

Boil a large pan of water and then turn it down to a gentle simmer. In batches, without letting them touch, place the bagels in the simmering water and cook for 1-2 minutes on each side. Drain and transfer to a tray lined with baking paper, spaced 5cm apart.

Brush each bagel with beaten egg or dairy-free milk, then top with the salty sesame mix.

Bake in the preheated oven for 20-22 minutes until golden brown, then allow to cool.

TO SERVE

Try topping them with salted butter, crumbled feta and a drizzle of honey; caramelised banana slices with crispy bacon; or smashed avocado with lime juice and chilli flakes.

Eating sensibly gives me more energy for an exercise-filled day and lets me sleep better. I love cooking and have found that I'm more aware of the need to look after my mental health since the pandemic, so it all ties together. I rely on fresh air and exercise – swimming, gymming, going out on my bike – as well as meeting up regularly with friends and surrounding myself with positive people.

JUDY MURRAY (@JUDYMURRAY_)

KEDGEREE

PREPARATION TIME: 10-15 MINUTES | COOKING TIME: 30 MINUTES | SERVES 2

INGREDIENTS

200ml oat or dairy milk

2 smoked haddock fillets, skin removed

1 onion, finely chopped

1 tbsp olive oil

1 tbsp curry powder

1 tsp ground turmeric

1 tsp ground coriander

1 tsp crushed fresh ginger

1 tsp crushed garlic

250g basmati rice

500ml stock

Salt and pepper

4 eggs

100g frozen peas

1 lemon, juiced

4 tbsp chopped fresh parsley

METHOD

Bring the milk to a simmer in a wide pan and poach the smoked haddock fillets for 7 minutes until cooked through.

Transfer to a plate and gently flake the fish when done.

Meanwhile, fry the chopped onion in the olive oil for 5 minutes until cooked through.

Add the spices, ginger and garlic to cook for another minute.

Stir in the rice, coating it with all the spices and aromatics, before pouring over the stock.

Season with salt and pepper, then put a lid on the pan and leave to cook for 12 minutes.

While the rice is cooking, boil the eggs for 6½-7 minutes.

Once cooked, run under cold water and then peel and halve or quarter each egg.

Once the rice is cooked through, stir in the flaked fish, frozen peas, lemon juice and parsley. Cook for another few minutes, then serve with the hard-boiled eggs on top.

I think good food has the power to nourish our bodies but also to bring us together around the table and hopefully make everyone feel supported and heard. I feel when I eat a balanced meal, my blood sugar levels are more stable, so my mood is too. Looking after your body through food filters down to your mental health.

MADELEINE SHAW (@MADELEINE_SHAW_)

CHAPTER
2

HAPPY GUT
HAPPY LIFE

This chapter focuses on healthy dishes that look after your gut, a crucial part of your body's overall health and wellbeing.

CUMIN ROASTED CAULIFLOWER & COUSCOUS SALAD

PREPARATION TIME: 10-25 MINUTES | COOKING TIME: 35 MINUTES | SERVES 4

INGREDIENTS

FOR THE SALAD

100g giant couscous

1 cauliflower, cut into bite-size florets

1 x 400g tin of chickpeas, drained

2 tsp ground cumin

1 tsp cumin seeds

Sea salt

Olive oil

1 lemon, juiced

Handful of mixed leaves

Handful of fresh coriander, chopped

Large handful of toasted pine nuts

FOR THE CORIANDER YOGHURT

Handful of fresh coriander, chopped

1 lemon, zested and juiced

200g natural yoghurt

1 tsp sumac

TO SERVE

100g feta

Toasted pine nuts

Fresh coriander, chopped

METHOD

Preheat the oven to 220°c/200°c fan/Gas Mark 7.

Cook the couscous according to the instructions on the packet. Once cooked, drain, rinse well and set aside until needed.

Place the cauliflower florets, drained chickpeas, ground cumin, cumin seeds, a pinch of salt and a good drizzle of olive oil into a large baking tray.

Mix well until all the cauliflower florets are coated in the oil, then roast in the preheated oven for 20 minutes.

Meanwhile, make the salad dressing. In a small bowl, combine the lemon juice with 2 tablespoons of olive oil and a pinch of salt.

Make the coriander yoghurt by mixing all the ingredients together in another small bowl.

Once the cauliflower and chickpeas have roasted, remove from the oven and spoon into a large bowl.

Add the prepared couscous, mixed leaves, chopped coriander and toasted pine nuts to the bowl, then pour in the dressing and mix well until everything is coated.

TO SERVE

Spoon the salad onto a large serving plate and crumble the feta over the top.

Finish with a sprinkle of pine nuts and some fresh coriander accompanied by the coriander yoghurt on the side.

My life's mission is to spread happiness to one billion people, which means addressing mental health issues too. To look after my own mental health, I take slow mornings and make my coffee with love. I also sit in silence for 30 minutes every day.

MO GAWDAT (@MO_GAWDAT)

CREAMY CARROT & RED LENTIL SOUP

PREPARATION TIME: 10-25 MINUTES | COOKING TIME: 30 MINUTES | SERVES 4

INGREDIENTS

FOR THE SOUP

Olive oil

1 red onion, peeled and diced

2 cloves of garlic, peeled and diced

2 carrots, peeled and chopped

3 sun-dried tomatoes, cut into small pieces

Pinch of salt

2 tsp smoked paprika

1 tsp brown rice miso paste

100g red lentils

1 tin of full-fat coconut milk

1 vegetable stock cube, mixed with 500ml boiling water

Dash of almond milk (optional)

TO SERVE

Natural yoghurt

Black pepper

Handful of fresh basil, chopped

METHOD

Place a large pan over a medium heat and add a drizzle of olive oil.

Once warm, add the diced onion, garlic, carrots, sun-dried tomatoes, and salt.

Mix well and cook for 10 minutes until the carrots and onions are soft.

At this point, add the smoked paprika and cook for 2 minutes before mixing through the rest of the ingredients.

Bring to a simmer, then leave to cook until the red lentils are soft which should take about 15-20 minutes.

Once the lentils soften, blend the whole mixture until smooth.

You may need to add a dash of almond milk until you reach the consistency you like best.

TO SERVE

Spoon the soup into bowls and pile high with natural yoghurt, a drizzle of olive oil, a twist of fresh black pepper and some chopped basil.

"

The best thing I can ever do for my mental health is to live in a way that makes me proud of me. That was always my biggest problem, because I didn't have a good relationship with myself, so making myself proud improves my self-esteem and so much flows from there.

BEN BIDWELL (@BENBIDWELL_THENAKEDPROFESSOR)

AROUND THE TABLE
– WITH –
ELLA MILLS

OVERCOMING CHALLENGES

Most of us will experience mental health challenges within our lives. The advent of everything I do now came with one of these challenges when I became very ill in 2011. I spent a few months in and out of hospital with a condition that meant my body could barely function and I had no life, no friends, nothing. Unsurprisingly, that had a huge impact on my mental health and it was my first experience of depression and anxiety. At that point, I also struggled with the vulnerability I needed to talk about or share it with others which I think massively exacerbated the depths of the lows I felt.

REFLECTION AND WELLBEING

I've been very lucky in my career to work within the wellbeing space and to be part of a generation who are encouraging everyone to talk about mental health in a really different way that's open, eloquent, vulnerable and emotionally intelligent. It is also increasingly easy to access daily tools to support our mental health; for me that's been yoga and meditation. They're the bedrock of my own day-to-day mental health support, creating the space and clarity I need to check in with my mind.

SHARING WITH OTHERS

Emotional literacy isn't something we're always taught in our culture and as a result we're not always able to show up in the way we really want to when people are struggling. We simply don't know what to say. I saw it so vividly when my mother-in-law passed away; so many people didn't say anything to my husband because they were scared to say the wrong thing and it simply furthered the sense of isolation. Moments like that have consistently highlighted the importance of collective connection to our emotions and as such our mental health.

PEOPLE INSPIRE PEOPLE

The more we're able to normalise the challenges that inevitably come with life – whether they're related to grief and loss, postpartum depression and anxiety, physical health, or anything else – the more connected we can feel. Having experienced aspects of each one of these challenges, I realise the importance of open conversations and of knowing how normal it is for our mental health to fluctuate. I feel incredibly lucky to have people in my life that I can talk to any time, any day.

GRILLED CORN, BLACK BEAN & SALSA VERDE TACOS

PREPARATION TIME: 10-15 MINUTES | COOKING TIME: 35-50 MINUTES | SERVES 3-4

INGREDIENTS

FOR THE SALSA VERDE

Large handful of fresh coriander

Large handful of fresh parsley

Large handful of fresh basil

2 cloves of garlic

2 tbsp capers

1 lime, juiced

Pinch of salt

Olive oil

FOR THE TACOS

2 corn on the cob

Olive oil

Sea salt

1 small red onion, peeled and chopped

2 cloves of garlic, peeled and chopped

300g cherry tomatoes, halved

2 tsp paprika

2 limes, juiced

2 x 400g tins of black beans, drained

8 small soft tacos

Handful of fresh coriander

METHOD

FOR THE SALSA VERDE

Finely chop the coriander, parsley, basil, garlic and capers.

Place into a bowl and mix through the lime juice, salt and a good drizzle of olive oil (we recommend 4-5 tablespoons of oil but it depends how many herbs you are using; you want the salsa to come together and form a sauce-like consistency).

Cover and place in the fridge until ready to use.

FOR THE TACOS

Preheat the oven to a medium heat on the grill setting.

Brush each corn cob with olive oil and sprinkle with salt.

Place the corn onto a baking tray and cook under the grill for 10-15 minutes until golden on the outside and cooked through.

Remove from the oven when done and slice the kernels off the cobs.

Meanwhile, place a large pan on a medium heat and add a drizzle of olive oil.

Once warm, add the chopped red onion, garlic and a pinch of salt. Mix well and cook for 5-10 minutes until the onions soften.

Add the cherry tomatoes and paprika to the pan. Mix well and cook for another 5 minutes until the tomatoes soften. Add the lime juice and drained black beans.

Mix again and cook for another 15-20 minutes until the black beans have softened, then turn the heat down low until ready to serve.

While the black bean mixture is cooking, warm up the soft tacos.

Once everything is ready, top the tacos with the black bean mixture, grilled corn kernels and a sprinkle of fresh coriander, then serve with the salsa verde.

I practice meditation to look after my mental health, which helps me stay more present. Time away from my phone and computer, with 24 hours offline each week, also helps with this. The more present I am the happier I am, but that's not always easy when you're prone to catastrophising. Cooking is a brilliant way of being more mindful: allowing yourself to focus just on the task at hand. There's something incredibly grounding about making a nourishing meal at home too.

ELLA MILLS (@ELLA.MILLS_)

MISO MUSHROOM DUMPLINGS

PREPARATION TIME: 20-35 MINUTES | COOKING TIME: 35 MINUTES | MAKES ABOUT 15

INGREDIENTS

500g chestnut mushrooms (or a mix of varieties)

1 onion, diced

2 leeks, finely sliced

3 cloves of garlic, diced

2 tsp brown rice miso paste

15 dumpling wrappers

Olive oil

Toasted sesame oil

Pinch of sesame seeds

METHOD

Cut all the mushrooms into small pieces, about the same size as a pea.

Place a large pan over a medium heat and add a drizzle of olive oil.

Once warm, add the onion, leeks, garlic, and a pinch of salt to the pan. Mix well and cook for 5-10 minutes, or until the onions and leeks turn soft.

Stir in the chopped mushrooms, mixing really well, and cook for 10-15 minutes, stirring every now and then to ensure nothing is sticking to the bottom of the pan.

Once the mushrooms have softened, mix through the miso paste and cook for another 5 minutes until everything is cooked through. Remove from the heat and set aside.

Once the mixture is cool, assemble the dumplings. There are two ways to do this:

1. Spoon 1 tablespoon of the mushroom filling into the centre of each dumpling wrapper. Hold the dumpling in one hand and close your hand to fold the dumpling together. Once the dumpling is in a V shape, pinch the sides together to seal. You can make little folds like traditional dumplings, or keep it simple by just sealing the outsides. You should be left with a little half-moon dumpling as shown in the photo.

2. For a slightly simpler way, spoon 1 tablespoon of the mushroom filling into the centre of each dumpling wrapper, then bring all the edges of the wrapper together in the middle, enclosing the filling. Pinch the top together and twist to seal. You should be left with a little round dumpling.

Repeat whichever process you prefer until you have assembled all the dumplings, then place them in the fridge until needed.

To cook the dumplings, heat a drizzle of toasted sesame oil in a pan over a medium heat. Once hot, add the dumplings to the pan and cook on each side for 2-4 minutes until golden and cooked through, adding a dash of water when you flip them.

Serve the dumplings immediately with a sprinkle of sesame seeds on top.

> Mental health is a lifelong journey, ever evolving, so the conversation about it should be never ending. Give up that cruel self-talk, it's toxic and doesn't serve anyone. Instead, do good stuff for others and make affirmations of kindness to yourself. I know that not moving my body and eating food that I haven't cooked affects my head and makes me sad. Bad habits like this are formed through fear, getting stuck. Breaking them is hard… but freedom awaits. Don't wait. You're SO worth a few broken windows: let the light in.
>
> LENA HEADEY (@IAMLENAHEADEY)

BAKED COD WITH
SPICY BUTTER BEAN STEW <u>&</u> OLIVE CRUMB

PREPARATION TIME: 10-15 MINUTES | COOKING TIME: 50-60 MINUTES | SERVES 4-5

INGREDIENTS

FOR THE TOPPING

2 slices of bread

5 black olives

Pinch of salt

50g grated parmesan

FOR THE STEW

Olive oil

1 red onion, peeled and diced

3 cloves of garlic, peeled and diced

400g tinned butter beans, drained

2 red peppers, cut into small chunks

2 tsp paprika

50g black olives, roughly chopped

400g tinned chopped tomatoes

1 vegetable stock cube (or stock pot) mixed with 300ml boiling water

1 heaped tbsp harissa paste

1 tbsp thick balsamic vinegar

30g grated parmesan

2 large skinless cod fillets (about 200-250g each), cut into 3 pieces each

Salt and pepper

METHOD

FOR THE TOPPING

Place the bread, olives and salt into a powerful blender and blend until you have a breadcrumb-like consistency.

Stir through the grated parmesan and place to one side.

FOR THE STEW

Place a large pan over a medium heat and add a drizzle of olive oil.

Once warm, add the onion, garlic and a pinch of salt.

Mix well and cook for 5-10 minutes, or until the onion turns soft.

At this point, add the butter beans, red pepper and paprika.

Mix well and cook for 5 more minutes before mixing through the olives, chopped tomatoes, vegetable stock, harissa paste, balsamic vinegar and grated parmesan.

Mix everything together and bring to the boil before reducing the heat and leaving to simmer for 20-25 minutes, or until the liquid has reduced to create a thick, flavoursome stew. You can always add a dash of water if the stew becomes too dry.

Meanwhile, preheat the oven to 210°c/190°c fan/Gas Mark 6½.

Once the stew is thick and delicious, place the cod fillets on top and scatter the breadcrumb topping over the fish and stew, then drizzle with olive oil.

Bake in the preheated oven for 20 minutes, or until the top turns golden and the fish has completely cooked through.

"

We all have a role to play in tackling mental health stigma. Suicide is preventable.
We don't have to be experts to play our part in creating mentally healthy cultures.

SIMON BLAKE (@SIMONABLAKE)

YOUR THOUGHTS AREN'T ALWAYS FACT.
TAKE A MOMENT TO STOP, BREATHE AND
REMEMBER WHAT IS REAL AND WHAT IS NOT.
SPEAK OPENLY WITH LOVED ONES
AND NEVER BE ASHAMED
TO SHOW YOUR EMOTIONS.

STEPHANIE ELSWOOD

BUTTERNUT SQUASH NOODLES WITH SATAY SAUCE & MISO MUSHROOMS

PREPARATION TIME: 30-45 MINUTES | COOKING TIME: 35 MINUTES | SERVES 4

INGREDIENTS

FOR THE MUSHROOMS

2 tbsp sesame oil

1 tbsp brown rice miso paste

1 tbsp maple syrup

1 tbsp brown rice vinegar

500g chestnut mushrooms, sliced

FOR THE NOODLES

100g frozen edamame beans

100g soba noodles

Drizzle of olive oil

300g butternut squash noodles (or 1 butternut squash, spiralised)

50g roasted peanuts

Sprinkle of sesame seeds

FOR THE SATAY SAUCE

3 tbsp smooth peanut butter

2 tbsp soy sauce (or tamari)

2 tbsp sesame oil

1 tbsp brown rice miso paste

1 tbsp brown rice vinegar

2 tsp maple syrup

1 lime, juiced

Pinch of salt

METHOD

FOR THE MUSHROOMS

In a small bowl, mix the sesame oil, brown rice miso paste, maple syrup and brown rice vinegar together until smooth.

Place the sliced mushrooms into a large bowl and pour over the miso marinade.

Mix well, cover and place in the fridge for at least 30 minutes.

Preheat the oven to 200°c/180°c fan/Gas Mark 4 and spread the marinated mushrooms on a baking tray, then cook for 25 minutes until tender.

FOR THE NOODLES

Place the frozen edamame beans in a small bowl and cover with boiling water. Leave for 5-10 minutes until they soften. At this point, drain and leave to one side until needed.

Prepare the soba noodles by placing a large pan of salted water over a medium heat. Once boiling, add the soba noodles and cook according to the timings on the packet, then drain and set aside.

Place a large frying pan or wok over a medium heat and add a drizzle of olive oil.

Once warm, add the butternut squash noodles. Mix well and cook for 5 minutes until they begin to soften.

Now stir in the soaked and drained edamame beans, then cook for another few minutes until the beans are heated through and the butternut squash noodles become tender.

FOR THE SATAY SAUCE

In a small bowl, mix all the ingredients for the satay sauce together until smooth.

Stir the satay sauce into the butternut squash noodles along with the soba noodles and roasted peanuts. Mix well and cook the whole dish for a few more minutes to heat everything through.

TO SERVE

Sprinkle the sesame seeds on top and the miso mushrooms either on the side, piled on top or mixed through the dish.

It is so important to have open and honest conversations about mental health; it could quite literally save someone. I practice yoga almost daily, I check in with how I am feeling regularly throughout the day, I speak to those closest to me, and I listen to my mind and body when it tells me to slow down. I have been on a journey of self-discovery to become more self-aware, and I feel so much better for it.

NIOMI SMART (@NIOMISMART)

CHICKEN, KEFIR & TURMERIC CURRY

PREPARATION TIME: 35-50 MINUTES, PLUS 4-8 HOURS MARINATING | COOKING TIME: 45 MINUTES | SERVES 4-6

INGREDIENTS

FOR THE MARINATED CHICKEN

500g kefir

3 cloves of garlic

2cm fresh turmeric

2cm fresh ginger

4 whole cloves

1 tsp garam masala

1 tsp salt

1kg skinless and boneless chicken thighs

FOR THE SAUCE

2 tbsp coconut oil

4 curry leaves

2 onions, finely sliced

1 green chilli, finely sliced

½ tsp ground turmeric

100g mango purée (from a can)

100g toasted desiccated coconut

Lime wedges (optional)

FOR THE TADKA

2 tbsp coconut oil

½ tsp cumin seeds

½ tsp brown mustard seeds

8 curry leaves

TO SERVE

Steamed basmati rice

Crispy fried shallots

Fresh coriander

METHOD

FOR THE MARINATED CHICKEN

Put 200g of kefir into a blender with the garlic, turmeric, ginger, cloves, garam masala and salt, then blend until smooth.

Cut the chicken into large chunks and place into a sealable bag.

Pour over the kefir marinade, seal the bag and massage into the chicken.

Place the chicken in the fridge for 4-8 hours to marinate.

When the chicken is ready, heat 1 tablespoon of the coconut oil for the sauce in a large sauté pan over a medium-high heat.

Drain the chicken, reserving the marinade, and fry until golden but not cooked through. Transfer to a plate.

FOR THE SAUCE

Add the coconut oil and the curry leaves to the pan.

Once they begin to pop, add the onions and sauté over a medium heat until soft, sweet and beginning to brown.

Stir in the chilli and cook for 1 minute, add the turmeric and stir to coat the onions.

Put the chicken back into the pan and reduce the heat to medium-low.

Add the reserved marinade, cover with a lid and simmer for 10-15 minutes or until the chicken is cooked.

Once the chicken is cooked, add the remaining 300g of kefir along with the mango purée and toasted coconut. Stir and heat to warm, then taste and season accordingly.

FOR THE TADKA

Heat the oil in a separate pan and add the spices. Once the seeds begin to pop, pour the hot tadka over the curry and stir through.

TO SERVE

Serve with the steamed rice, crispy fried shallots and a sprinkle of chopped coriander.

> Try not to get too worried about stressful situations; it's amazing how time and a little patience can work out many problems almost by themselves. When it comes to looking after my own mental health, yoga and a bit of gardening give me time away from stress and collectively help me find balance.
>
> JAMES LOHAN

THE
IRONBRIDGE
GORGE MUSEUM

CKIG 17

JP 17
Sunset at Coalport China Museum
Coalport China Museum

WILD RICE, ROASTED AUBERGINE & SWEET POTATO SALAD

PREPARATION TIME: 10-25 MINUTES | COOKING TIME: 35 MINUTES | SERVES 4

INGREDIENTS

FOR THE SALAD

5 baby aubergines, quartered

1 large sweet potato, cut into bite-size chunks

Olive oil

Sea salt

100g wild rice

150g brown rice (you can use red rice or any other kind you have)

150g toasted walnuts, roughly chopped

Large handful of parsley, finely chopped

FOR THE DRESSING

1 orange, zested and juiced

2 tbsp red wine vinegar

2 tbsp olive oil

2 tsp honey

1 tsp sumac

TO SERVE

Handful of chopped parsley

METHOD

Preheat the oven to 210°c/190°c fan/Gas Mark 6½.

Place the aubergine and sweet potato onto a large baking tray with a drizzle of olive oil and a pinch of salt.

Mix well until all the vegetables are coated in oil, then roast in the preheated oven for 25-30 minutes, or until softened.

Once cooked, remove from the oven and set aside.

Meanwhile, cook the rice according to the instructions on the packets and make the dressing by mixing all the ingredients together with a good pinch of salt.

Once the rice has cooked, drain any excess water and spoon the rice into a large bowl.

Pour in the dressing and mix well until all the grains are coated.

Add the roasted vegetables, chopped walnuts and parsley to the bowl and mix again until everything comes together.

TO SERVE

Spoon the salad onto a large serving plate and top with some fresh parsley.

"
It is now more important than ever to encourage people to talk openly about their feelings and to know that is it okay to ask for help, as well as how to find support. For me, the best thing to do if I am feeling stressed is to get outside and spend time in nature. I find it particularly helpful if I can do this in mindful silence, as my senses are soothed by the sights, scents and sounds that we do not always notice if talking or listening to podcasts or music.

AMELIA FREER (@AMELIAFREER)

AROUND THE TABLE
– WITH –
CATHERINE TYLDESLEY

A STORYLINE TO RAISE AWARENESS

I've been a strong advocate of raising mental health awareness for quite a few years which was inspired by a storyline we did, when I was part of Coronation Street, about male suicide. At the time, I think we all knew somebody who had taken their own life or been affected by suicide. We started working with different charities in this space and it opened up a new world for me because I suddenly realised how bad things were, particularly for men aged between 18 and 35. Once that storyline had gone out, calls to those mental health charities increased significantly in the space of five days so it was amazing to see the impact that storyline had on viewers and to know that we could make such a difference.

FOOD IS THE BEST MEDICINE

When I was struggling with my own mood and hormones, I read Anxiety and Depression by Dale Pinnock about nutrition for mental health and it just blew me away that there's so much that can really help us. For example, low Vitamin D levels are directly linked to depression and anxiety, which can be helped by supplements and spending more time outside. To me, these little tips are absolutely priceless and I truly believe in using food to help combat stress and raise serotonin levels, working from the inside out to give your mental and physical health the best possible shot.

FEEDING THE FAMILY

An emphasis on home cooking is something I grew up with because my parents are amazing cooks. They got me involved in the kitchen from an early age, which I'm really grateful for. My husband and I practise the same with our son; we started growing our own vegetables a couple of years ago and seeing that journey for him has been absolutely joyous. Don't get me wrong, we love a treat here and there, but we're also super passionate about looking after our physical and mental health through the food we eat on a daily basis.

THE POWER OF MEDITATION

I was introduced to meditation at drama school and it is still a big part of my daily life. I realised I could stand in the wings just before going on stage, be in my own bubble and feel calm through meditation. Sometimes it was an effort to get to that place but the more I practised, the easier it got. Over the years, meditation has been something I would dip into when I needed, but when I fell pregnant with my first child, I started hypnobirthing which involved meditating each day. It's stuck since then and I always try to make time for meditation because it just resets and calms my mind in a very busy world.

ROASTED AUBERGINE, RED PEPPER & PRAWN PEARL BARLEY

PREPARATION TIME: 10-25 MINUTES | COOKING TIME: 45 MINUTES | SERVES 4

INGREDIENTS

FOR THE PEARL BARLEY

1 large aubergine, cut into bite-size chunks

1 red onion, peeled and thinly sliced

1 red pepper, sliced

1 vegetable stock cube

600ml boiling water

100g pearl barley

100g risotto rice (or brown/paella rice)

200g raw king prawns, peeled

Olive oil

Salt and pepper

FOR THE PASTE

2 red peppers, cut into chunks

2 cloves of garlic, peeled

2 tbsp olive oil

1 tbsp harissa paste

2 tsp smoked paprika

1 lime, juiced

Pinch of salt

TO SERVE

Black pepper

Handful of fresh parsley, chopped

METHOD

Preheat the oven to 210°c/190°c fan/Gas Mark 6½.

Place the aubergine chunks onto a large baking tray, drizzle with olive oil, add a large pinch of salt and then cook for 30-35 minutes, or until the aubergine turns soft. Remove from the oven and set aside.

Place all the paste ingredients into a blender and blend until a smooth mixture forms.

Place a large wide pan over a medium heat and add a drizzle of olive oil.

Once warm, add the sliced red onion and a pinch of salt, mix well and cook for 5-10 minutes until the onion softens.

Add the sliced red pepper and cook for 5 minutes before adding the red pepper paste. Mix everything together before leaving it to simmer for 5 minutes while you dissolve the stock cube in the boiling water.

After 5 minutes, mix through half of the hot stock along with the pearl barley and rice.

Give everything a thorough stir and bring to the boil, then reduce the heat to a simmer. Add the rest of the stock bit by bit as needed, cooking until the pearl barley and rice have softened and absorbed all the liquid. Make sure you wait until all the liquid has been absorbed before adding the next portion of stock, only doing this as and when you feel the dish needs more liquid. This should take around 20-30 minutes in total.

Fold the prawns into the pearl barley and rice mixture.

Cook over a medium-high heat for around 5-10 minutes until the prawns are completely cooked through, then mix in the roasted aubergines.

TO SERVE

Divide the aubergine, red pepper and prawn pearl barley between bowls and serve with some fresh black pepper and chopped parsley on top.

> Meditation has become a big part of my life and I practice most days. I also enjoy sound therapy and love to walk: trekking or outdoor swimming is my happy place! I love to take comfort food recipes and make them healthier. Healthy gut = healthy mind!
>
> CATHERINE TYLDESLEY (@AUNTIECATH17)

CREAMY SALMON & NEW POTATO CURRY

PREPARATION TIME: 10-25 MINUTES | COOKING TIME: 35 MINUTES | SERVES 4-6

INGREDIENTS

FOR THE CURRY

600g new potatoes, halved (or sweet potatoes)

Olive oil

Sea salt

1 onion, peeled and diced

2 cloves of garlic, peeled and diced

1 tbsp curry powder

1 x 400g tin of coconut milk

150ml water

Large handful of fresh spinach

4 salmon fillets, skinned, deboned and cut into bite-size chunks

FOR THE CURRY PASTE

2 limes, juiced

1 tsp paprika

1 tsp ground turmeric

1 x 340g tin of sweetcorn, drained

TO SERVE

Pinch of chilli flakes

Handful of fresh coriander, chopped

Cooked brown rice

2 limes, cut into wedges

METHOD

Preheat the oven to 240°c/220°c fan/Gas Mark 9.

On a large baking tray, mix the new potatoes with a good drizzle of olive oil and a pinch of salt. Roast for 25 minutes until crispy on the outside and soft on the inside.

Once cooked, remove from the oven and set aside until needed.

Place a large pan over a medium heat and add a drizzle of olive oil.

Once warm, add the diced onion, garlic and a pinch of salt. Mix well and cook for 5-10 minutes, or until the onions soften.

Meanwhile, make the curry paste by placing the lime juice, paprika, turmeric, drained sweetcorn and a pinch of salt into a food processor or blender.

Blend until the mixture comes together to create a smooth paste.

Add the curry powder to the onion and garlic, mix well and cook for a few seconds before stirring through the curry paste, followed by the coconut milk and water.

Bring the mixture together before leaving on a low simmer for 10 minutes.

Mix the potatoes and spinach through the curry and cook until the spinach has wilted.

Gently stir the salmon through the curry, then bring it to the boil before covering with a lid and cooking for 6-10 minutes, or until the salmon is just cooked through, ensuring you don't overdo the fish.

TO SERVE

Top with a pinch of chilli flakes and a handful of fresh coriander. Serve with cooked brown rice and lime wedges on the side.

As the father of two daughters, I want them to grow up understanding that being vulnerable will never make them weak, it will only show their strength and ability to be their authentic selves. Talking things through with friends and family is a necessity for looking after my mental health and has become easier as I realise that it was only myself who ever made it difficult. It doesn't matter if you feel like you're boring people, just talk and let people know that you aren't okay.

DAN CADAN

MIXED BEAN BURGERS WITH KIMCHI RELISH

PREPARATION TIME: 10-25 MINUTES | COOKING TIME: 1 HOUR 5 MINUTES | MAKES 4 BURGERS

INGREDIENTS

FOR THE BURGERS

4 portobello mushrooms

1 red onion, peeled and diced

2 cloves of garlic, peeled and diced

1 tsp ground cumin

1 tsp smoked paprika

1 tin of butter beans, drained and rinsed

1 tin of black beans, drained and rinsed

2 tbsp plain flour

1 tsp brown rice miso paste

Pinch of salt

Olive oil

FOR THE KIMCHI RELISH

200g kimchi

100g natural yoghurt

1 tsp brown rice miso paste

1 tsp sugar

Pinch of salt

TO SERVE

4 burger buns, halved

2 large vine tomatoes, sliced

1 lettuce, end removed

METHOD

FOR THE BURGERS

Cut the mushrooms into small chunks.

Place a large pan over a medium heat and add a drizzle of olive oil.

Once warm, add the onion, garlic and a pinch of salt. Mix well and cook for 5-10 minutes until the onion becomes soft.

Once the onion softens, add the spices and mix through.

Cook for another minute before adding the chopped mushrooms.

Mix everything together well and leave to cook for another 10 minutes until the mushrooms reduce in size and soften.

Stir through the drained butter beans and leave to cook for 10 minutes. After 10 minutes the butter beans should be soft enough to crush with the back of a wooden spoon or a fork. Crush the butter beans into the mixture to create an almost paste-like consistency.

Finally, stir through the drained black beans, plain flour and miso paste. Cook for a further 10 minutes before leaving the mixture to cool down.

Once the mixture feels firm enough to shape, weigh and divide it into 4 patties of around 150g each. Shape the patties into burger shapes using your hands.

You can cook them straight away or cover them and leave them in the fridge until needed.

FOR THE KIMCHI RELISH

Place all of the ingredients into a powerful blender and blend until smooth.

Once the mixture comes together, cover and place it to one side until needed.

TO SERVE

Heat a large pan over a medium heat. Add a drizzle of olive oil, then add the burgers and cook on each side for 5-6 minutes until charred.

You can also place them in an oven at 200°c/180°c fan/Gas Mark 6 for 10-15 minutes.

Serve the burgers in buns with sliced tomatoes, lettuce and the kimchi relish.

TURKEY, LEMONGRASS & GINGER MEATBALLS

PREPARATION TIME: 25-40 MINUTES | COOKING TIME: 15 MINUTES | SERVES 4

INGREDIENTS

FOR THE SLAW

200ml apple cider vinegar

100ml water

1 tsp fine salt

1 tbsp caster sugar

300g white cabbage, shredded

3 carrots, peeled into strips

150g radishes, finely sliced

¼ small bunch of coriander, leaves picked

FOR THE MEATBALLS

400g turkey mince

3 tbsp dried breadcrumbs

2 tbsp grated fresh ginger

1 lemongrass stalk, finely chopped

½ small bunch of coriander, finely chopped

½ tsp chilli flakes

Sea salt and black pepper

1 tbsp sesame oil

TO SERVE

Sriracha

4 flatbreads

METHOD

FOR THE SLAW

Put the vinegar, water, salt and sugar into a large saucepan, bring to the boil and simmer for 1 minute until the sugar dissolves.

Add the cabbage, carrot and radish and stir to combine.

Leave to cool for 20 minutes, stirring occasionally to coat all the vegetables, then drain once cool and stir in the coriander leaves.

FOR THE MEATBALLS

Put the turkey mince, breadcrumbs, ginger, lemongrass, coriander and chilli flakes into a bowl along with a good pinch of salt and a twist of black pepper.

Mix well to combine, then shape the mince into 14-16 meatballs of around 30g each.

Heat the sesame oil in a large non-stick frying pan, add the meatballs and fry for 12-14 minutes until they are golden brown and cooked through, then cut one open to check before taking them off the heat.

TO SERVE

Serve the meatballs on a pile of the pickled slaw, along with a drizzle of sriracha over the top, if you like, and a flatbread.

Everyone looks after their mental health in different way so don't feel like you're ever doing it wrong. Don't be afraid to ask for help, or speak to people to lighten your load, as everyone is feeling the same, trust me!

HANNAH COCKROFT (@HLCMBE)

TURMERIC FISH STEW WITH BULGUR WHEAT SALAD

PREPARATION TIME: 15-30 MINUTES | COOKING TIME: 30-35 MINUTES | SERVES 4

INGREDIENTS

FOR THE STEW

1 tbsp olive oil
1 red onion, chopped
Thumb-size piece of ginger, grated
2 cloves of garlic, chopped
1 red chilli, sliced
1 fish stock cube
2 tsp ground cumin
1 tsp each ground coriander, cinnamon and turmeric
1 tbsp tomato purée
1 tsp harissa
1 orange, zested
10-15 cherry tomatoes
1 large tomato, sliced
2 tbsp ground almonds
1 tbsp fish tagine paste
1 tin of butter beans, drained
500g cod or monkfish, cubed

FOR THE SALAD

190g bulgur wheat
1 vegetable stock cube
2 tbsp flaked almonds
Handful of radishes, sliced
Handful of dried apricots, sliced
Handful of sun-dried tomatoes
Handful of fresh parsley, chopped
1 pomegranate (seeds only)
1 orange, juiced

METHOD

FOR THE STEW

Heat the olive oil in a large saucepan and cook the onion over a medium heat until golden, then stir in the ginger, garlic and chilli.

Meanwhile, dissolve the fish stock cube in 600ml of boiling water.

Add the ground spices and a pinch of salt to the pan, cook for 1 minute, then add the tomato purée, harissa, orange zest and fresh tomatoes.

Give everything a mix for 2 minutes, stir in the ground almonds and fish tagine paste.

Pour in the fish stock you prepared earlier and the butter beans.

Place the lid on and leave to cook for 20 minutes on a low heat.

FOR THE SALAD

Measure the bulgur wheat into a mug and then make up twice that amount of stock with boiling water and the vegetable stock cube.

Add the bulgur and stock to a saucepan with a pinch of salt and cook on a medium heat for 15 minutes.

Toast the almonds in a dry pan on a low heat until golden and combine the remaining ingredients in a large bowl.

Mix in the cooked bulgur wheat and toss until everything is combined and dressed in the orange juice. Finish by scattering the toasted almonds and more fresh parsley on top.

TO FINISH

Add the cod or monkfish to the stew and simmer for 3-5 minutes until just done.

Serve the stew over the bulgur wheat salad and enjoy!

Looking after our mental health is easier said than done. For me, exercise offers a release for my mind and body. I nourish my body with food which I know will support me, and I remind myself to be kind to myself, which a lot of the time we can forget to do. I have also loved to cook since I was little. As a very active person, I find that cooking allows me to draw my focus to one thing amidst the busyness of my day. It is time purely for me.

SARAH ANN MACKLIN (@SARAHANNMACKLIN)

CHAPTER
3

FAST FOOD
(BUT NOT AS YOU KNOW IT)

This chapter is packed with a range of international recipes which can be made when you're short on time.

SALMON POKE BOWL

PREPARATION TIME: 5-10 MINUTES | COOKING TIME: 30 MINUTES | SERVES 2

INGREDIENTS

FOR THE SOY GLAZED SALMON

2 tbsp rice wine vinegar

2 tbsp soy sauce

1 tbsp sesame oil

1 tbsp brown sugar

2 skinless salmon fillets (preferably fresh from a fishmonger)

FOR THE POKE BOWL

250g cooked rice

1 large carrot, peeled

4 tbsp pickled red cabbage, drained

6 radishes, finely sliced

75g edamame beans, podded or mange tout, halved lengthways

2 tsp black sesame seeds

METHOD

In a small bowl, mix the vinegar, soy sauce, sesame oil and brown sugar until combined. Pour half of this glaze into another bowl and set aside.

Cut the salmon into cubes and place into one bowl of the marinade, then leave to cure for 30 minutes.

Toss the remaining soy glaze through the cooked rice and divide between two bowls.

If you're using a packet of pre-cooked rice, put it in a sieve and pour some boiling water over it first to loosen and break up the grains.

Peel the carrot into ribbons and divide between the two bowls on top of the rice. Arrange the pickled cabbage, radishes, edamame beans or mange tout and raw salmon cubes in sections on the rice to create a colourful, vibrant topping.

Sprinkle over the black sesame seeds, serve and enjoy!

"

Exercise, a routine and good food really help with my mental health. I like to know my plan for each week, whether that's training, meals, events with family and friends or 'me time'. It helps me manage my time and, in turn, my mental health so things don't get on top of me. I also love spending time in the kitchen! At the end of a training day, I look forward to grabbing a few ingredients and getting lost in a recipe.

GEORGIA TAYLOR-BROWN (@GEORGIATB)

SWEETCORN RIBS WITH CASHEW AIOLI SAUCE

PREPARATION TIME: 10-25 MINUTES | COOKING TIME: 40 MINUTES | SERVES 2

INGREDIENTS

FOR THE SWEETCORN RIBS

2 corn on the cob

3 tbsp olive oil

2 tsp smoked paprika

1 tsp sumac

Pinch of sea salt flakes

Pinch of chilli flakes

FOR THE CASHEW AIOLI

150g cashews

100ml almond milk

1 clove of garlic, peeled

1 lemon, juiced

1 tsp Dijon mustard

Pinch of salt

Pinch of paprika

METHOD

Preheat the oven to 210°c/190°c fan/Gas Mark 6½.

Place the cashews into a small bowl and cover with boiling water.

Leave for at least 10 minutes to soften.

FOR THE SWEETCORN RIBS

Halve the corn cobs lengthways down the middle, then again so you have 4 ribs from each cob. This is usually easiest starting at the top and cutting the whole way down.

Place the sweetcorn ribs onto a large baking tray and make the rub by mixing the olive oil, smoked paprika and sumac together in a small bowl.

Brush this rub over the sweetcorn until completely coated before topping each piece with a sprinkle of sea salt flakes.

Cook in the preheated oven for 30-35 minutes, or until the corn pieces have curled up a little and turned golden on the outside.

FOR THE CASHEW AIOLI

Drain the cashews and place into a blender along with all the other ingredients.

Blend until smooth and creamy, adding a dash more almond milk if needed.

TO SERVE

Place the sweetcorn ribs onto a serving plate and sprinkle with chilli flakes.

Spoon the cashew aioli into a small bowl with a pinch of paprika on top to serve.

> Try not to take on board what people who don't know you say about you. If they are being negative, chances are they are projecting their own insecurities and issues. If they are being positive then this is great but don't let that get to your head or distract you from your goals.
>
> LAWRENCE OKOLIE (@LAWRENCEOKOLIE)

COURGETTE & RICOTTA CROSTINI

PREPARATION TIME: 5-20 MINUTES | COOKING TIME: 10 MINUTES | SERVES 2 (AS A LIGHT LUNCH OR SNACK)

INGREDIENTS

1 courgette

125g ricotta

2 tbsp finely grated parmesan

Sea salt and black pepper

Olive oil

1 baguette, cut diagonally into 4 slices

1 clove of garlic, halved

½ lemon, zested and juiced

½ tsp Dijon mustard

Handful of basil leaves, finely shredded

METHOD

Cut the courgette on the diagonal into approximately 0.5cm slices.

In a small bowl, mix the ricotta with the parmesan and season with salt and pepper.

Put a griddle pan on a medium-high heat and brush with olive oil, then cook the courgette slices in the hot pan for a couple of minutes on each side, until softened and charred.

Meanwhile, grill or toast the baguette slices on both sides until golden brown.

Drizzle them with olive oil and rub with the cut garlic clove, then place on a plate.

In a large bowl, whisk 2 tablespoons of olive oil with the lemon zest and juice, mustard and shredded basil. Season this dressing generously to taste with salt and pepper.

Add the griddled courgette to the bowl and toss to coat.

TO SERVE

Spread each toasted baguette slice with a quarter of the ricotta mixture, then top with the warm lemony courgette.

You can also garnish with extra basil, lemon zest and parmesan if you like.

"

I am not a great cook, but I love the generous nature of cooking for others and eating together. I also read books, laugh with friends, think of others first, sleep when I am tired and spend as much time as possible outside to look after my mental health. Remember that the world is full of kind people and nothing lasts forever.

DAME JOANNA LUMLEY

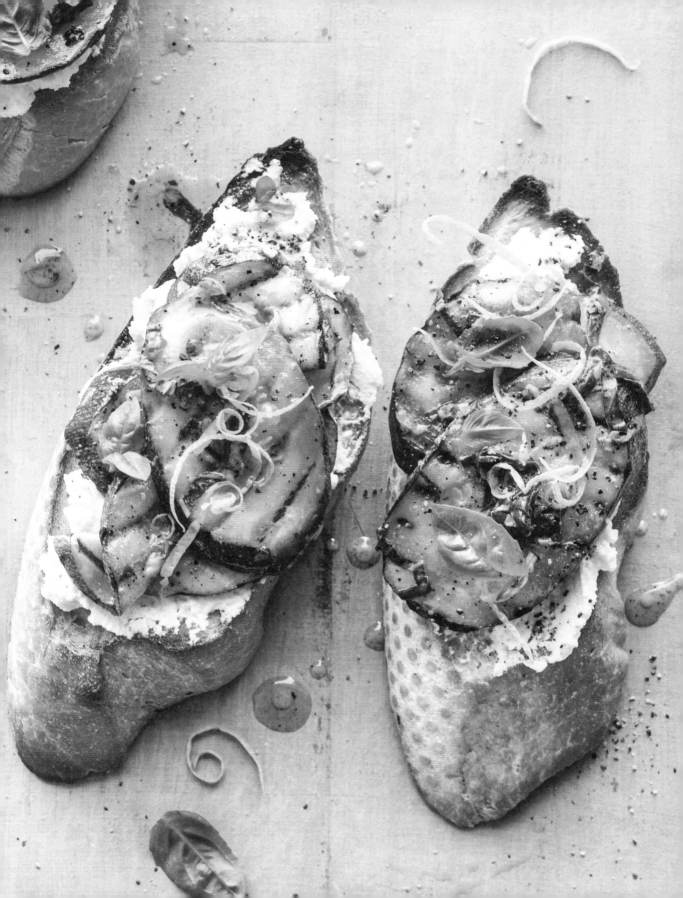

HENRY FRASER

FROM PHYSICAL TO MENTAL STRENGTH

When it comes to mental health, I've been at extreme ends of the spectrum. When I was 17 and on holiday with my friends, I dived into the sea and hit my head on the undulating seabed, dislocating the fourth vertebrae in my neck and leaving me unable to move anything below that. Prior to my accident, I was a very anxious person but mental health was something I'd never considered until suddenly my physical capabilities were completely gone. I've had to move that strength up into my head and retrain my mind to think in a completely different way. Even with the huge physical limitations I have now, my world is far more open because I refocused my attitude towards life. Of course, those things haven't happened overnight – it takes a lot of time and patience, just like physical training. Eventually, the negative thoughts really do fade away and once you come out the other side, things are brighter than you ever thought possible.

MAKING ART

I'd always loved art as a child but it wasn't until years after my accident that I found an app on the iPad that I could use by holding a stylus in my mouth and drawing on the touch screen. Drawing took my mind off being stuck in bed and, looking back, it was definitely a form of mindfulness. I had to concentrate so heavily and intently on what I was doing that in that moment there were no other thoughts in my head. My painting has really progressed and the challenge still keeps me focused, wanting to do more and be better. It's also brought me back to the same love and joy I had as a kid for making art and just being in that creative space.

POSITIVE THINKING

When I started working for Pembrokeshire Rugby Club, the CEO at the time asked if I'd ever thought about sharing my story in a room full of people. I had entertained the thought, but as a teenager I was too anxious to get up in front of a class of 12 or 14 people. I decided to give it a go and experienced this huge rush of adrenaline and relief the moment I finished the talk. I now go into situations thinking about the best outcomes rather than being terrified of the worst thanks to the confidence public speaking has given me.

ADVERSITY CAN BE A GIFT

Adversity has allowed me to think and live very differently and do things I never even dreamed of. I truly believe that everyone has it in them to get through tough times, I guess because I've been on both sides of that wall. If we're unflinching, determined and patient with ourselves, we can get through it. It takes time, it takes effort, and it can be disheartening when you're not seeing results every day but that ability to dig deep is in all of us.

SPRING GREEN SPAGHETTI

PREPARATION TIME: 5-20 MINUTES | COOKING TIME: 15-20 MINUTES | SERVES 2

INGREDIENTS

180g spaghetti

1 tbsp olive oil

1 clove of garlic, finely chopped

1 leek, finely sliced (approx. 100g)

Sea salt and black pepper

100g asparagus spears

70g fresh or frozen peas

70g fresh or frozen broad beans

2 large handfuls of mixed soft herbs
(e.g. dill, mint, parsley, chives and basil)

100g crème fraiche

1 tsp Dijon mustard

½ lemon, zested and juiced

Parmesan or vegetarian hard cheese

METHOD

Bring a large pan of water to the boil, salt it heavily, then add the spaghetti and cook for 1 minute less than the packet suggests.

Meanwhile, in a large frying pan or casserole dish with a lid, heat the olive oil over a medium heat.

Add the garlic and leek along with a pinch of salt and cook for 5-7 minutes, until soft.

Slice the asparagus spears diagonally into roughly 3-4cm pieces, cutting any harder ends into smaller rounds about 1cm thick.

Add these to the leeks along with a ladleful of pasta water, then put the lid on and allow to steam for around 5 minutes, until tender.

After about 2 minutes, add the peas and broad beans and continue to cook with the lid on. Meanwhile, chop all the soft herbs.

Drain your pasta, reserving some of the cooking water.

Transfer the spaghetti into the pan with the vegetables and stir or toss to combine.

Turn the heat down very low and stir in the crème fraiche, mustard, lemon zest, lemon juice and nearly all the chopped herbs, along with a splash of the reserved pasta water to loosen the mixture and create a sauce.

Taste and season with salt and pepper, plus an extra squeeze of lemon juice if needed.

If the sauce is looking claggy and dry, add more pasta water and continue tossing until the spaghetti is thoroughly coated and the sauce looks silky.

TO SERVE

Using a pair of tongs, divide the pasta between two bowls.

Sprinkle with the remaining herbs and finish with a grating of fresh parmesan or vegetarian hard cheese.

"

Personally, I practice a lot of gratitude and live in each moment, enjoying the smallest things so that my day is full of positives no matter how small they might seem. I do this so that if something negative does happen it does not have a big impact on my day.

HENRY FRASER (@HENRYFRASER0)

HONEY BAKED HALLOUMI SHAWARMA WITH MINTY YOGHURT DRESSING

PREPARATION TIME: 5-20 MINUTES | COOKING TIME: 40 MINUTES | SERVES 4

INGREDIENTS

FOR THE DRESSING

200g natural yoghurt

30g fresh mint, chopped

1 tsp runny honey

½ lemon, juiced

FOR THE HALLOUMI

4 tbsp olive oil

2 tbsp runny honey

1 tbsp tamari

1 tbsp dried oregano

½ lemon, juiced

Pinch of salt

2 blocks of halloumi (about 200g each)

TO SERVE

4 warm wraps

4 large vine tomatoes, sliced

1 lettuce, ends removed

Handful of pomegranate seeds

Hummus

Lemon wedges

METHOD

Preheat the oven to 200°c/180°c fan/Gas Mark 6.

FOR THE DRESSING

Place all the ingredients into a bowl and stir until it comes together. This dressing is even better the next day, so you can make it ahead.

FOR THE HALLOUMI

In a small bowl, mix the oil, honey, tamari and oregano and salt together.

Score each block of halloumi into slices diagonally from the top to the bottom, ensuring not to cut the whole way through (I make about 5 cuts in each block).

Place the halloumi into a lined baking dish and pour over the oil and honey mixture, making sure the whole block is coated including between the cuts.

Bake the halloumi in the preheated oven for 35-40 minutes, or until golden on the outside and soft on the inside.

Once the halloumi is cooked, remove from the oven and transfer to a sharing dish.

TO SERVE

Serve the baked halloumi with the minty yoghurt dressing and some warm wraps, sliced tomatoes, lettuce, pomegranate seeds, hummus and lemon wedges to squeeze over the top.

"

I love to cook with my kids – it's a lovely bonding experience – and exercise to look after my mental health. Be kind to yourself and recognise that no one has all the answers; we are all works in progress.

NATALIE PINKHAM (@NATALIE_PINKHAM)

CHARRED CHICKEN PITAS WITH LEMONY SALSA VERDE

PREPARATION TIME: 15-30 MINUTES | COOKING TIME: 15 MINUTES | SERVES 4

INGREDIENTS

FOR THE SALSA VERDE

Small bunch of fresh basil

Small bunch of fresh parsley

2 cloves of garlic, roughly chopped

2 lemons, zested and juiced

5 anchovies

4 tsp capers

1 tsp chilli flakes

5 tbsp olive oil

1-2 tbsp cold water

FOR THE CHICKEN

½ tsp paprika

¼ tsp cayenne pepper

2 tbsp olive oil

2 chicken breasts

4 pitas or flatbreads

2 handfuls of salad leaves

4 tbsp pickled red cabbage or onion, drained

METHOD

FOR THE SALSA VERDE

Put all the ingredients except the oil and water into a blender and blitz until finely chopped. Add the oil and water, then blitz again until you have a dressing consistency.

FOR THE CHICKEN

Mix the paprika, cayenne, and a big pinch of flaky sea salt with the olive oil.

Put the chicken breasts between two sheets of greaseproof paper and bash them with a rolling pin until they're around 1cm thick.

Remove the top sheet of greaseproof and massage the chicken with the spiced oil.

Heat a large frying pan or griddle over a high heat and, once hot, add the chicken.

Fry for 4-5 minutes on either side, making sure you don't move it, so it gets a nice colour. Turn down the heat slightly and continue to cook for another few minutes until it's cooked all the way through.

Meanwhile, heat the pitas or flatbreads either in a toaster or in the microwave.

Slice to create a pocket or use one side of the flatbread and fill with salad leaves and pickled red cabbage.

Cut the cooked chicken breasts on an angle, then divide between the pitas and drizzle over the salsa verde.

> Cycling significantly supports my mental health and gives me the ability to connect with others while spending time outside in nature, which are both extremely important for me. Cooking has also been something that has helped me look after my mental health. It allows me to separate myself from work and I love enjoying a meal that I've prepared for my family after a long day. It's not just about the process but also the time it gives me to spend with friends and family.
>
> LUKE BOASE (@LUCKYSAINT_LUKE)

TALK TO SOMEONE.
WHEN YOU CAN'T TALK, WRITE IT DOWN.
DON'T LEAVE THINGS IN YOUR HEAD.
PUT THEM INTO WORDS.

DR JULIE SMITH

MISO HAKE PARCELS

PREPARATION TIME: 15-30 MINUTES | COOKING TIME: 15 MINUTES | SERVES 4

INGREDIENTS

50g butter, softened

5cm fresh ginger, grated

1 tbsp miso paste

1 lime, zested and halved

100g spinach

4 hake fillets (or any white fish)

3 spring onions, finely sliced

½ red chilli, finely sliced

TO SERVE

Sesame seeds

Steamed rice

Green vegetables

METHOD

Preheat the oven to 200°c/180°c fan/Gas Mark 6.

In a small bowl, combine the softened butter with the grated ginger, miso paste, lime zest, and lime juice from one half.

Stir to form a kind of paste – it will look a bit lumpy, but don't worry as the butter will melt properly when cooked.

Cut 4 x 30cm squares of baking paper and place on a work surface.

In the centre of each one, place a handful of spinach leaves the same length as your hake fillet, to form a kind of bed, then place a hake fillet on top.

Spread 1 heaped teaspoon of the miso butter over each fillet.

Top with the sliced spring onions and chilli, then wrap up the baking paper so that it forms a parcel where steam can't escape.

To do this, transfer the baking paper to a baking tray and bring the long sides together in the centre, covering the fish, and then fold the paper over at the top to create a seal. Do this twice, then repeat at the short ends. If they don't stay folded, use a toothpick to secure the paper, or you can make the fold underneath the fish to keep it sealed.

Bake the hake parcels in the oven for 15 minutes, until the fish is just cooked through.

TO SERVE

Unwrap and sprinkle with a handful of sesame seeds, then slide everything off the paper and plate up alongside the steamed rice and green vegetbles such as pak choi, green beans or broccoli.

Squeeze over the remaining lime juice, if you like.

> I think it's vital that we normalise the conversation about mental health and suicide. I try my best to live my life simply, with love and gratitude, to look after my own mental health. I find that cooking allows me time to switch off and focus on something that I can achieve while giving pleasure to others.
>
> JAMIE THEAKSTON (@JAMIE.THEAKSTON)

BROCCOLI PESTO PASTA

PREPARATION TIME: 5-20 MINUTES | COOKING TIME: 20 MINUTES | SERVES 4

INGREDIENTS

FOR THE PASTA

1 large head of broccoli, cut into florets

400g pasta (rigatoni or fusilli)

Large handful of spinach

Handful of toasted pine nuts

FOR THE PESTO

150g cashews

150ml water

50ml olive oil

50g parmesan, grated

Bunch of fresh basil (about 30g)

1 clove of garlic, peeled

1 lemon, juiced

Pinch of salt

TO SERVE

Pine nuts

Parmesan

Black pepper

METHOD

Place a large pan of water over a medium heat and add a pinch of salt.

Once the water is boiling, add the broccoli florets and cook for 3-4 minutes, or until they soften but still have a slight bite.

Remove the broccoli from the pan using a slotted spoon and rinse under cold water.

Put half of the broccoli into a food processor and add the rest of the pesto ingredients. Blend until everything comes together to form a smooth, creamy pesto and set aside.

Cook the pasta in the pan of boiling water for 1 minute less than stated on the packet. Drain, saving some of the water, then put the pasta back in the pan over a medium heat.

Add the remaining broccoli, spinach, pine nuts and pesto to the pasta.

Cook for 5 minutes until everything is piping hot and the spinach has wilted.

Stir in a dash of pasta water, if needed, to get a really creamy texture.

TO SERVE

Place the pasta into bowls and top with some pine nuts, grated parmesan and freshly ground black pepper.

> The main thing that helps my mental health is focusing on one thing (like a recipe) at a time, which allows me to remove those daily distractions, calm my mind, and slow everything down a little.
>
> LEANNE HAINSBY (@LEANNEHAINSBY)

CHICKEN JALFREZI

PREPARATION TIME: 10-25 MINUTES | COOKING TIME: 45-50 MINUTES | SERVES 4

INGREDIENTS

FOR THE SPICE PASTE

2 tsp cumin seeds

I tsp coriander seeds

I tsp brown mustard seeds

I tsp ground fenugreek

I tsp ground turmeric

½ tsp salt

½ small bunch of coriander

2 green chillies, roughly chopped

3 cloves of garlic, peeled

5cm fresh ginger, peeled

2 tbsp tomato purée

2 tbsp vegetable oil

FOR THE CURRY

2 tbsp vegetable oil

2 green peppers, cut into chunks

I large onion, finely chopped

4 free-range skinless and boneless chicken thighs, cut into chunks

4 large tomatoes, chopped

½ lemon, juiced

TO SERVE

Basmati rice or naan

Coriander leaves, to garnish

METHOD

FOR THE SPICE PASTE

In a large frying pan or wok on a medium-high heat, toast the cumin, coriander and mustard seeds for a few minutes until smelling fragrant.

Remove from the pan and add these into a food processor with all the remaining ingredients and blend until smooth.

FOR THE CURRY

Heat the oil in the same pan used to toast the spices and then add the peppers.

Fry for a few minutes on a high heat until the peppers are browning, then turn the heat down to medium-high and add the onion.

Cook for around 5 minutes, stirring occasionally, until soft.

Add the chicken and cook for a further 5 minutes.

Spoon the spice paste into the pan and stir so it coats everything.

Cook for a few minutes, then add 250ml of water.

Turn the heat down to low-medium and simmer for 10-15 minutes until the sauce is looking thicker.

Add the chopped tomatoes and simmer for a further 15 minutes.

Stir the lemon juice into the curry, then taste and season with more salt, if needed.

TO SERVE

Serve with fresh coriander leaves scattered on top and rice or naan on the side.

I'm a big believer in the need for separation when it comes to stress management. Cooking requires concentration, but also separation from other tasks, and the focus on the activity itself can be therapeutic. Food has the power to bring people together. It can break down barriers and help form connections. Connection is the single most important factor to better support our collective mental health.

HARRY CORIN (@HARRY.CORIN)

DR JULIE SMITH

WORKING IN MENTAL HEALTH

Many people think that being a clinical psychologist would make you less likely to experience mental health problems. But the job itself can put an incredible strain on your wellbeing. You are sedentary, often working in isolation, working with people in distress and listening to first-hand accounts of traumatic experiences. In the first few years after qualifying, I learned to compartmentalise my day so that I could be present in my personal life as well as my professional life. I wouldn't say I completely leave work at work. I often think of my clients and wonder how they are doing but it has helped me to look after my own wellbeing when working with complex trauma.

BACK TO BASICS

If you don't keep tabs on your wellness through self-reflection, you are less likely to pick up on early signs that your mental health is fluctuating. Going back to basics makes a big difference. I keep an eye on how I am eating, my sleep, exercise and social contact because they all help to keep me at my best. When I am not feeling great, I can almost guarantee that one of those factors has slipped from my routine. I also make a conscious effort to limit my time spent online. It is a huge part of my work now, so I try to put my phone down as much as possible when I'm with my family.

LEANING ON OTHERS

Whenever I have faced difficult times outside of the clinical work, my husband Matt has been my sounding board. We've known each other since we were kids and are best friends, so he is my go-to. I am also fortunate enough to have a lovely family and a few good friends that want the best for me. Having one or two people in your life that you can trust and lean on for support is crucial and makes all the difference when it comes to facing difficult times. Working on social media has also given me a great opportunity to meet some brilliant individuals who have been so generous with their knowledge and advice.

IF I COULD TALK TO MY YOUNGER SELF...

I would say, make that radical decision to do the absolute best by yourself. Be the voice you need to hear. Treat yourself how you want others to treat you. Don't wait for an offer of help, start asking for it. Turn your focus from one of inward judgement to one of outward curiosity and don't forget to prioritise simple joys.

STICKY PRAWNS WITH VEG-PACKED EGG FRIED RICE

PREPARATION TIME: 5-20 MINUTES | COOKING TIME: 15-20 MINUTES | SERVES 4

INGREDIENTS

250g jasmine or long grain rice

4-5 tbsp sesame oil

330g raw king prawns

6 spring onions, sliced and separated into white and green parts

1 x 330g bag of pre-prepared stir fry vegetables

3 tbsp soy sauce

4 medium eggs, beaten

3 cloves of garlic, finely grated

25g fresh ginger, peeled and finely grated

3 tbsp sriracha

1 tsp honey

TO SERVE

Sesame seeds

Soy sauce and sriracha

METHOD

Rinse and cook the rice according to the instructions on the packet, then drain and rinse thoroughly under cold water to get rid of any starch. Set aside to cool.

In a large wok, heat 1 tablespoon of sesame oil and fry the prawns on a medium-high heat for a minute or two on each side, until just turned pink.

Transfer to a plate or bowl and set aside for later.

Return the wok to a high heat and add 2 tablespoons of sesame oil.

Sprinkle in the white parts of the spring onions and the pack of vegetables.

Fry for a few minutes to soften, then add the rice and 2 tablespoons of soy sauce.

Cook this mixture for a few minutes, stirring often to coat the rice with the soy sauce. Now move the rice and vegetables to the sides of the wok, add a drizzle of oil and pour in the beaten eggs.

Leave for a minute before beating again, then stir vigorously through the rice so that the egg breaks up among the grains.

Add a pinch of salt and most of the green sliced spring onions (reserving a handful for garnish) to the pan, then turn the heat down very low while you make the sauce for the prawns.

Heat another tablespoon of oil in a clean frying pan over a medium-high heat, then add the finely grated garlic and ginger.

Cook for a couple of minutes, stirring so it doesn't burn, until just beginning to colour.

Now add the sriracha, honey and remaining soy sauce.

Let it all sizzle for a few minutes, stirring occasionally, until looking sticky.

Add the prawns and gently shake the pan to coat. Once coated, turn down the heat.

TO SERVE

Divide the egg fried rice between 4 bowls and top each one with the sticky glazed prawns, a sprinkling of sesame seeds, a splash of soy sauce and sriracha, then the remaining green spring onion slices.

"

I try to keep a clear sense of what matters most to me, so that when life steers me away from those things I can stop, re-evaluate, and make decisions based on my values. I also look after the foundations for good mental and physical health: sleep, nutrition, exercise and social connection. If we let those things slide, we become vulnerable, so I always keep them in mind.

DR JULIE SMITH (@DRJULIE)

CRISPY CHICKEN & COCONUT NOODLES

PREPARATION TIME: 15-30 MINUTES | COOKING TIME: 25 MINUTES | SERVES 2

INGREDIENTS

FOR THE NOODLES

1 tbsp vegetable oil

3 cloves of garlic, minced

4 spring onions, finely sliced

5cm fresh ginger, grated

1 tbsp tomato paste

½ tsp gochugaru or chilli flakes

400ml tinned coconut milk

1 tbsp soy sauce

2 pak choi, halved lengthways

2 packets dried ramen (180g)

FOR THE CRISPY CHICKEN

2 chicken breasts

40g plain flour

1 egg, beaten

50g panko breadcrumbs

2 tbsp vegetable oil

TO SERVE

Jammy soft-boiled eggs, halved

Spring onions, finely chopped

Sesame seeds

Chilli flakes

Chilli oil

METHOD

FOR THE NOODLES

Put the oil into a medium saucepan over a medium heat and add the garlic, spring onions and ginger. Fry for 1-2 minutes until fragrant and starting to soften.

Add in the tomato paste and gochugaru or chilli flakes and cook for 30 seconds.

Pour in the coconut milk, soy sauce and 250ml of boiling water and stir to combine, then take off the heat and set aside until needed.

FOR THE CRISPY CHICKEN

Put the chicken breasts between two sheets of parchment and bash with a rolling pin to flatten until they are an even 1-2cm thickness.

Put the flour, egg and breadcrumbs into 3 separate bowls.

Season the chicken breasts with salt and then dip them into the flour, then the beaten egg and finally the breadcrumbs until fully coated.

Heat the oil in a large non-stick frying pan and fry the breadcrumbed chicken for 5-6 minutes on either side until golden brown and cooked through.

FOR THE NOODLES

Once the chicken is almost cooked, bring the coconut milk broth you made earlier to the boil and then turn the heat down to a simmer.

Add the pak choi and ramen, then cover and simmer for 3-4 minutes, stirring occasionally until the pak choi is soft but still has a bite and the ramen is cooked.

TO SERVE

Slice the crispy chicken diagonally into strips.

Ladle the ramen noodles, pak choi and broth into bowls, place the chicken on top and finish with your desired toppings such as soft-boiled eggs and spring onions.

Sprinkle over some sesame seeds and chilli flakes, then drizzle with chilli oil if you like.

If I could give my younger self some advice, it would be: 1) The unwelcome visitor always leaves. 2) Try and ride it out. 3) Don't self-medicate. 4) Talk to anyone who will listen. These days I look after my mental health by staying sober, nurturing my marriage, and eating well. That last one doesn't cure depression but eating badly does compound it.

DENISE WELCH (@DENISE_WELCH)

CRISPY TEMPEH TACOS

PREPARATION TIME: 10-25 MINUTES | COOKING TIME: 35 MINUTES | SERVES 4

INGREDIENTS

FOR THE TACOS

400g chestnut mushrooms (or a mix)

1 onion, peeled and diced

3 cloves of garlic, peeled and diced

2 tsp smoked paprika

1 x 400g tin of black beans, drained

300g ready-to-eat smoked tempeh, cut into small pieces

2 tbsp tahini

1 tbsp harissa paste

1 lime, juiced

2 tsp brown rice miso paste

12-16 taco shells

Salt and pepper

Olive oil

TO SERVE

Guacamole

Plain yoghurt

Pinch of chilli flakes

Handful of fresh coriander, chopped

Hot sauce

METHOD

Chop the mushrooms into roughly pea-sized pieces.

Place a large pan over a medium heat and add a drizzle of olive oil.

Once warm, add the diced onion, garlic and a pinch of salt.

Mix well and cook for 10 minutes until soft.

Once the onion softens, add the paprika and mix well.

Cook out the spice for a minute or two before adding the chopped mushrooms.

Mix really well and cook for 10-15 minutes, stirring regularly to ensure nothing is sticking to the bottom of the pan.

Once the mushrooms have softened, mix in the drained black beans and tempeh, then cook for another 5-10 minutes to soften.

Stir through the tahini, harissa, lime juice and brown rice miso paste.

Leave the mixture cooking on a low-medium heat while you prepare the taco shells according to the instructions on the packet.

TO SERVE

Serve up a big bowl of the mushroom filling alongside the taco shells and guacamole, plain yoghurt, chilli flakes, chopped coriander and your favourite hot sauce to build them as you like.

I believe eating the right foods can be like taking medicine. Cooking connects you to this process. Alongside a good diet and training, I practice meditation and open communication to look after my mental health. My advice to others would be to be patient, be gentle with yourself and speak openly to people.

LOUI BLAKE (@LOUI_BLAKE)

ZA'ATAR CHICKEN WITH HERBY BULGUR SALAD & HARISSA YOGHURT

PREPARATION TIME: 5-20 MINUTES | COOKING TIME: 45-60 MINUTES | SERVES 2

INGREDIENTS

FOR THE CHICKEN

3 tbsp olive oil

1 tbsp lemon juice

1 tbsp za'atar

1 clove of garlic, crushed

Sea salt and black pepper

4 free-range chicken thighs (skin on)

FOR THE BULGUR SALAD

100g bulgur wheat

1 tbsp olive oil

1 tbsp lemon juice

½ small bunch of mint leaves, chopped

½ small bunch of parsley, chopped

½ small bunch of chives, chopped

FOR THE HARISSA YOGHURT

100g natural yoghurt

2 tsp rose harissa paste

METHOD

Preheat the oven to 200°c/180°c fan/Gas Mark 6.

FOR THE CHICKEN

Mix the olive oil, lemon juice, za'atar and garlic together in a bowl with some salt and pepper, then rub thoroughly over the chicken thighs.

Sprinkle each thigh with sea salt flakes, then roast in the preheated oven for 30-40 minutes until thoroughly cooked. To test this, pierce the thickest part of the meat with a skewer and make sure the juices run clear.

FOR THE BULGAR SALAD AND HARISSA YOGHURT

Put the bulgur wheat in a small saucepan, cover with boiling water and cook on a medium-high heat for 15 minutes with the lid on. Drain and set aside to cool when done.

In a small bowl, season the yoghurt with salt and pepper and then stir in the harissa paste. Chill in the fridge until the chicken is ready.

Put the cooled bulgur wheat into a large bowl and add the olive oil, lemon juice, chopped herbs, a generous pinch of sea salt and a good twist of black pepper.

Stir until thoroughly combined.

TO SERVE

Spoon some of the herby bulgur salad onto two plates, then place two chicken thighs on each and drizzle over some of the cooking juices.

Give the harissa yoghurt a good stir and then drizzle over the top.

If I could give my younger self some advice, it would be keep running, keep talking and don't care what people think. If something makes you happy and hurts no one, you don't need to explain it.

JASON FLEMYNG

IT'S OKAY TO FEEL HOW YOU FEEL.
YOU DON'T HAVE TO HAVE IT ALL
FIGURED OUT YET AND YOU DON'T HAVE
TO COMPARE YOURSELF TO ANYONE ELSE.

FOCUS ON WHAT REALLY MAKES YOU HAPPY,
AND NOT ABOUT WHAT LOOKS COOL TO OTHERS.

LEANNE HAINSBY

STARTER'S ORDERS WRAP

PREPARATION TIME: 10-25 MINUTES | COOKING TIME: 25 MINUTES | SERVES 4

INGREDIENTS

2 sweet potatoes

1 tbsp olive oil

2 tsp cumin seeds

Sea salt and black pepper

250g ready-cooked lentils

200g cherry tomatoes, halved

1 red pepper, deseeded and sliced

2 handfuls of spinach or mixed baby leaves

4 raw spinach or wholemeal tortilla wraps

FOR THE PESTO

1 clove of garlic

75g fresh basil leaves

50g pine nuts

50g parmesan, grated

150ml extra virgin olive oil

METHOD

Preheat the oven to 180°c/160°c fan/Gas Mark 4.

Cut the sweet potatoes into chip shapes and spread out in a roasting tin.

Drizzle over the olive oil and scatter over the cumin seeds.

Season with salt and pepper to taste, then roast for 25 minutes until beginning to caramelise around the edges.

Meanwhile, put all the ingredients for the pesto into a food processor and pulse to combine, or chop by hand, leaving some texture.

Lay out the roast sweet potatoes, cooked lentils, cherry tomatoes, red pepper, leaves and pesto alongside the tortilla wraps and make up the wraps as you wish.

> If you are struggling, ask family or friends for help. I kept my struggles to myself for a long time and wish I'd spoken out sooner as they would have been there for me. I've learnt that it's important not to take on too much and to be able to say no. I think keeping fit physically is a key part of looking after your mental wellbeing too. I also try to fit some 'Me Time' into my day, whether that's with friends or a candlelit bath and music where I can completely switch off from day-to-day pressures.
>
> DAME KELLY HOLMES (@DAMEKELLYHOLMES)

VIETNAMESE STYLE STICKY SHAKING BEEF

PREPARATION TIME: 30-45 MINUTES | COOKING TIME: 5 MINUTES | SERVES 2

INGREDIENTS

500g rump steak, cut into bite-size cubes

2 red onions, finely sliced

1 tbsp cornflour, mixed to a paste with 1 tbsp water

FOR THE MARINADE

2 cloves of garlic, finely chopped

1 tbsp dark soy sauce

1 tbsp fish sauce

2 tsp sugar

1 tsp ground black pepper

FOR THE SAUCE

4 tbsp white wine vinegar

4 tbsp oyster sauce

4 tbsp water

1 tbsp sugar

TO SERVE

Cooked rice of your choice

1 lime, cut into wedges

METHOD

Put the beef into a bowl with the marinade ingredients.

Stir well and then set aside for 20 minutes.

Meanwhile, combine the sauce ingredients in a small bowl and set aside.

Heat a splash of oil in a non-stick frying pan over a high heat.

When hot, add the marinated beef. Stir fry for 2 minutes until it begins to caramelise.

Now add three quarters of the sliced onions to the pan and stir fry for 1 minute.

Pour in the sauce and cook for a further 2 minutes.

Turn down the heat and quickly stir in the cornflour paste to thicken the sauce, making sure there are no lumps.

Once ready, serve the sticky beef with rice and the remaining red onion scattered on top, placing the lime wedges on the side for squeezing over.

"

If I could give my younger self some advice about looking after my mental health, it would be to talk. Don't bottle things up. Exercising and talking to people are what help me now. Cooking is my passion though; I find it therapeutic and also find great enjoyment in sharing food with others.

CHRIS BABER (@CHRISBABER)

VULNERABILITY IS STRENGTH
AND THE MORE WE CAN OPENLY
SHARE OUR STRUGGLES,
THE MORE CONNECTED AND
SUPPORTED WE OFTEN FEEL.

ELLA MILLS

TUNA CEVICHE

PREPARATION TIME: 30-45 MINUTES | SERVES 2

INGREDIENTS

½ small red onion, very finely chopped

Sea salt

Caster sugar

220-250g fresh sashimi-grade tuna

½ green chilli, very finely chopped (red chilli works too, if you like it hot)

1 lime, juiced

2 handfuls (approx. 10-15g) of coriander leaves, finely chopped

½ ripe avocado, cubed

Corn tortilla chips or tostadas

METHOD

Put the finely chopped red onion in a bowl, sprinkle over two good pinches of sea salt and a pinch of sugar, then set aside while you prepare the tuna.

Dice the tuna into 2cm cubes.

Add the tuna to the red onion along with the finely chopped chilli and the lime juice.

Stir to coat everything evenly, then cover and leave in the fridge for 20 minutes.

After 20 minutes, remove the bowl from the fridge. By now the tuna will have been partially cooked by the lime juice and will look white-grey around the edges.

Stir in the chopped coriander and avocado until combined.

Taste the ceviche and season with more salt and lime juice, if necessary.

Serve with tostadas or tortilla chips.

"

If I could give my younger self some advice about looking after one's mental health, it would be don't be afraid to talk.

TOM PARKER BOWLES

CRAB, CHILLI & LEMON PASTA WITH PANGRATTATO

PREPARATION TIME: 10-25 MINUTES | COOKING TIME: 10 MINUTES | SERVES 2

INGREDIENTS

180g pasta (orecchiette, spaghetti or linguine)

2 tbsp olive oil

2 cloves of garlic, finely chopped

1 large slice of crusty bread, blitzed into breadcrumbs using a food processor

Salt and black pepper

½ red chilli, deseeded and finely chopped

100g fresh cooked crab meat

1 lemon, half zested and juiced, the other half cut into wedges

½ small bunch of flat-leaf parsley, finely chopped

METHOD

Bring a large saucepan of water to the boil, salt it heavily, then add the pasta and cook according to the instructions on the packet.

FOR THE PANGRATTATO

Heat 1 tablespoon of the olive oil in a large frying pan over a medium heat.

Add half of the garlic and cook for 1-2 minutes.

Now stir in the breadcrumbs along with a big pinch of salt and black pepper.

Turn up the heat to medium-high and fry for about 3-4 minutes, stirring constantly, until toasted and golden.

Transfer to a bowl and set aside to cool slightly.

Wipe the pan clean with kitchen paper or a cloth.

FOR THE PASTA

Put the frying pan back onto a medium heat with the remaining olive oil.

Add the rest of the garlic and cook while stirring for a couple of minutes until the garlic is turning golden (but not brown).

Add the chilli and cook for another minute.

Turn the heat down very low and add the crab, along with the lemon juice and a handful of the chopped parsley.

Drain your pasta and add it to the pan, stirring to combine everything.

TO SERVE

Add the lemon zest and remaining chopped parsley to the cooled pangrattato and give it a stir, then you're ready to serve up.

Divide the crab pasta between two bowls, top with the pangrattato and a wedge of lemon on the side for squeezing over the pasta, if desired.

> Admitting to mental struggles feels like acknowledging a weakness, yet most of us suffer with them to a greater or lesser degree at points in our lives and it is vital to talk and seek help when needed. I try to have some moments in each day when I'm not rushing around, and I find that cooking is a good way to release stresses as well as a natural break between work and downtime.
>
> HATTA BYNG (@HATTABYNG)

CHAPTER
4

SOUL FOOD

This chapter is full of family favourites
and mouth-watering recipes for
everyone's favourite dishes.

AUBERGINE PARMIGIANA

PREPARATION TIME: 10-25 MINUTES | COOKING TIME: 50-75 MINUTES | SERVES 3-4

INGREDIENTS

Olive oil

1 red onion, finely chopped

3 cloves of garlic, finely chopped

Sprinkle of chilli flakes

2 x 400g tins of chopped tomatoes

1 tsp oregano

Handful of fresh basil, chopped

1 tbsp thick balsamic vinegar

Sea salt and black pepper

3 large aubergines, cut into 5mm slices lengthways

75g parmesan, grated

100g mozzarella, sliced

Fresh basil leaves

METHOD

Preheat the oven to 220°c/200°c fan/Gas Mark 7.

Heat a little olive oil in a saucepan over a medium heat and fry the onion for 5-10 minutes until soft and translucent.

Add the garlic and a sprinkle of chilli flakes and continue to cook for a further minute.

Add the chopped tomatoes followed by the oregano, fresh basil and balsamic.

Season generously with sea salt and black pepper, then bring to the boil.

Reduce the heat and simmer for 20-25 minutes, or until the sauce has thickened.

Meanwhile, pour some olive oil into a small dish and using a pastry brush, generously brush the aubergine slices with oil on each side.

Heat a large frying pan over a medium heat and fry the slices in batches for about 4-5 minutes until softened and lightly browned on both sides. Be careful to not let the pan get too hot or the aubergine will char before cooking through.

Once cooked, transfer the aubergine to a plate lined with kitchen paper before repeating the process with the next batch.

Spread one third of the tomato sauce over the bottom of a baking dish and sprinkle with parmesan.

Lay half the aubergine slices on top, tightly and evenly packed, then add another sprinkle of parmesan. Repeat with the next third of tomato sauce, the remaining aubergines and more parmesan before finishing with a final layer of tomato sauce.

Top with the remaining parmesan, sliced mozzarella and a few fresh basil leaves.

Bake in the preheated oven for 30 minutes or until the tomato sauce is bubbling and the cheese has melted and browned.

Remove from the oven and allow to cool for 5 minutes before topping with some fresh basil leaves and black pepper.

I'm a huge believer in the power of sleep, hydration, and exercise. I go through phases with meditation, but the two things that have really helped me recently are therapy and breathwork. I believe in what Beder stands for and in the positive mental health impact of delicious food.

ELIZABETH DAY (@ELIZABDAY)

STICKY KOREAN BEEF RIBS

PREPARATION TIME: 20 MINUTES, PLUS 2-12 HOURS MARINATING | COOKING TIME: 3 HOURS 30 MINUTES | SERVES 4

INGREDIENTS

4 cloves of garlic, peeled and grated

10g fresh ginger, peeled and grated

100g gochujang

60ml soy sauce

60ml rice wine or mirin

6 tbsp dark brown sugar

2 tbsp chilli flakes (preferably Korean)

1 tbsp sesame oil

4 beef short ribs (approx. 3kg)

TO SERVE

Sesame seeds

Spring onion, sliced

METHOD

Mix all the ingredients together except the ribs to make a marinade.

Pour this into a large roasting tin, then add the ribs meat side down and make sure they're well coated with the marinade.

Cover the tray with cling film and leave to marinate for at least a couple of hours, or overnight if possible.

Preheat the oven to 170°c/150°c fan/Gas Mark 3.

Sear the marinated ribs in a hot pan with a little oil to get some colour on the outside, then transfer them back to the roasting tin and add 100ml of water.

Re-cover the roasting tin with foil and cook the ribs in the oven for 3 hours, until the meat is falling off the bone.

Once cooked, remove the ribs from the oven and carefully pour all the marinade and juices from the roasting tin into a saucepan.

Turn the ribs over so they are meat side up and set the grill to a high heat.

Place the saucepan of marinade over a high heat and bubble until thickened, which should take about 10 minutes. Spoon the sauce over the ribs and slide them under the hot grill.

Cook for 5-7 minutes until the ribs are caramelised, basting them halfway through.

TO SERVE

Serve the ribs and scatter with sesame seeds and sliced spring onion.

> One of the most transformational things anyone ever told me about mental health was that emotions aren't enemies, they're just your brain telling you to feel a certain way to process a situation. The only way these feelings ever go away is if we feel them, so taking time to check in with how we're doing and allowing ourselves to feel our emotions is a powerful tool for staying mentally healthy.
>
> BEN WEST (@IAMBENWEST)

SEAFOOD JAMBALAYA

PREPARATION TIME: 10-15 MINUTES | COOKING TIME: 1 HOUR | SERVES 4-6

INGREDIENTS

3 tbsp rapeseed oil

1 large onion, finely chopped

2 sticks of celery, finely chopped

4 cloves of garlic, minced

1 green pepper, finely sliced

200g andouille sausage or chorizo, sliced (if using chorizo, reduce the amount of smoked paprika by half)

2 tbsp tomato purée

1 tbsp sweet paprika

1 tbsp smoked paprika

1 tsp cayenne pepper

1 tsp cracked black pepper

1 tbsp chopped fresh thyme

1 tbsp Worcestershire sauce

200g long grain rice

1 tin of chopped tomatoes

400g chicken stock

1 tsp salt

4 langoustines

300g mussels, cleaned

300g king prawns

1 squid tube, cut into rings

Lime wedges, to serve

METHOD

Heat the oil over a medium heat in a large pan, then sweat the onion and celery for 8-10 minutes or until soft and sweet with no colour.

Add the garlic and cook for 1 minute before adding the green pepper and sausage.

Turn up the heat and brown for 2-3 minutes.

Stir in the tomato purée and spices.

Cook for 2 minutes, then add the fresh thyme and Worcestershire sauce.

Add the rice and cook for 1-2 minutes, stirring to coat all the grains.

Add the chopped tomatoes and stock, along with the salt, then bring the sauce to a simmer and cover with a lid. Cook gently for 15 minutes.

Remove the lid and mix in all the seafood.

Add some more stock if the sauce looks dry.

Cover with the lid again and simmer for 10 minutes or until the seafood is pink, the shells have opened and the rice is pretty much cooked.

Remove the pan from the heat and let it stand for 5-10 minutes, during which time the rice will continue to plump and swell.

Taste, adjust the seasoning and squeeze over some fresh lime juice before serving.

"

I cook most of the evening meals in my house and see it as extremely therapeutic. It forces me to slow down and be present, from preparing all the vegetables right through to the creative process of combining all the ingredients…but the best bit is of course in the eating. I feed my soul as well as my stomach!

LAWRENCE PRICE (@LAWRENCEPRICE_)

SOUTHERN FRIED CHICKEN BURGER

PREPARATION TIME: 30-45 MINUTES, PLUS MARINATING OVERNIGHT | COOKING TIME: 15 MINUTES | SERVES 4

INGREDIENTS

4 skinless and boneless chicken thighs
500ml buttermilk
1 tsp salt
1 egg
100g milk
75g rice flour
30g cornflour
2 chicken stock cubes*
1 tsp paprika
100g cornflakes, blitzed*
Oil for deep frying

FOR THE DRESSING

1 gherkin, finely chopped
½ shallot, finely chopped
2 tbsp mayonnaise
2 tbsp ketchup
1 tsp Dijon mustard
1 tsp sugar
½ tsp lemon juice
½ tsp cracked black pepper
3 drops of Worcestershire sauce*

TO SERVE

Burger buns*
Garnishes of your choice
*Gluten-free options available

METHOD

Coat the chicken thighs with the buttermilk and salt in a bowl.

Cover and allow to marinate in the fridge overnight.

Whisk the egg and milk together in one bowl.

Combine the rice flour, cornflour, crumbled stock cubes and paprika in a second bowl.

Place the blitzed cornflakes in a third bowl.

Remove the chicken from the buttermilk and let it drip dry before coating in the seasoned flour mixture, then the egg mixture, and finally the cornflakes.

Lay the chicken on a tray, then dip each piece once again into the egg mixture and then the cornflakes. This ensures a really crispy crust.

Heat the oil for deep frying to 140°c and fry the chicken in batches for 8 minutes, then set on a wire rack to drain.

Now heat the oil to 180°c and refry the chicken for 2-3 minutes or until golden and crisp.

Drain on kitchen paper and sprinkle with a little extra salt while hot.

FOR THE DRESSING

Mix all the dressing ingredients together in a small bowl and set aside in the fridge.

TO SERVE

Serve the fried chicken in burger buns filled with the dressing and garnishes of your choice such as lettuce, tomato, cheese and gherkins.

I have been suffering heavily with my mental health over the last year or so, to the point of having thoughts that are tough to handle. In order to change, I have switched my thought process on the purpose of life, which I now consider to be life itself. Don't allow your mind to tell you stupid things when you get older. Stay the course and remember that life is just about living and having fun. Everything else is just part of the process.

KIERON WEBB (@KIERON_WEBB)

LETTING GO OF WORRY

I used to be a terrible worrier and it completely drains you. Only worry about the things you can do something about. I appreciate that's easier said than done but don't worry about things you can't influence. You have no time machine; you can't turn the clock back. What you can do is ask yourself whether there's anything you can do to rectify the situation and the lesson it's given you.

MENTAL HEALTH IN BUSINESS

When I started my business, I would really get involved with the colleagues I was responsible for and we'd have events, conferences, overseas trips – anything we enjoyed outside the normal trajectory of what we were doing in our business lives. They became more than just colleagues and that was key. In the business today, we recently doubled the number of mental health first aiders because it's great for the people involved to be able to give back, and to make sure there's a touchpoint for everybody in the organisation that's much closer than a website or a telephone call.

MUSIC FOR YOUR MIND

I find that music can stimulate and change your mindset for the day. Years ago, if I had to go to a presentation or a meeting with lots of people, I would get incredibly nervous – my mouth would be as dry as cardboard and my heart rate would soar – so I would use music to get myself going. I only listen to upbeat music for that kind of thing, what I call sunny songs, because no matter how you're feeling and what else is happening, they can change your whole attitude.

WHAT MAKES US HUMAN

I'm still a very insular individual and very rarely share. Everything's my problem and everything is on my shoulders. So, lots of the things that I personally do to enhance my mental wellbeing are self-taught and picked up from my own experiences. I make no apology for all those things sounding so simple and so basic – I'm not giving you a magic bullet, because there isn't such a thing. It's a whole combination of things that everybody can do. That's what makes us human.

TARO WITH PORK

PREPARATION TIME: 15-30 MINUTES | COOKING TIME: 1 HOUR 45 MINUTES | SERVES 6

INGREDIENTS

100ml olive oil

1.4kg shoulder of pork, trimmed and cut into 5cm chunks

1 large onion, peeled and diced

2kg taro (kolokassi), peeled and wiped

2 tbsp tomato purée

1.5 litres water

1 lemon, juiced

Salt and pepper

METHOD

Place a large pan over a medium heat and add the olive oil.

Once warm, add the pork and fry for 15-20 minutes, or until browned on all sides.

During this time, stir occasionally to ensure the pork doesn't stick to the bottom of the pan. Once cooked, remove the pork and set aside.

Put the diced onion into the pan with a pinch of salt.

Mix well and cook for 5-10 minutes until soft.

Break off pieces of the taro and add these to the pan.

Mix well and cook for 5-10 minutes until browned on all sides. At this point, stir through the tomato purée and cook for a few more minutes.

Return the pork to the pan and season with salt and pepper.

Pour over the water and bring to a simmer, then add the lemon juice and stir everything.

Cover with a lid and simmer for 1 hour, or until the pork is tender.

Serve with some fresh herbs sprinkled on top and some slices of bread.

> No matter how quickly things are going in life, take time to be in the moment and enjoy or learn from those experiences. I like to keep active and exercise most days. A reflective walk with my dog can often help clear the mind and help me to refocus. Music and friends are a good tonic too.
>
> THEO PAPHITIS (@THEOPAPHITIS)

KEEMA WITH PEAS & ROTI

PREPARATION TIME: 10-25 MINUTES, PLUS 30 MINUTES RESTING | COOKING TIME: 1 HOUR 15 MINUTES | SERVES 4

INGREDIENTS

FOR THE ROTI

300g atta flour (or wholewheat bread flour, sieved to remove husks)

1 tsp fine salt

120g ghee, melted and cooled (or oil)

245ml lukewarm water

FOR THE KEEMA

2 tbsp ghee

3 cardamom pods

1 cinnamon stick

2 bay leaves

1 onion, finely chopped

3 cloves of garlic, grated

25g (thumb-sized piece) fresh ginger, grated

1 tbsp each ground cumin and ground coriander

½ tsp ground turmeric

800g lamb mince

400g tinned plum tomatoes

100g frozen petit pois

1 tsp garam masala

1 green chilli, sliced

Yoghurt, to serve

METHOD

FOR THE ROTI

Add the flour and salt to your mixing bowl, make a well in the centre and add 2 tablespoons of the ghee with the water.

Use your hand to combine them and make a sticky dough.

Tip onto a lightly floured surface and knead for about 7-10 minutes until smooth.

Clean and lightly oil the bowl, then put the dough back in, cover and set aside for at least 30 minutes.

FOR THE KEEMA

Melt the ghee in a large frying pan over a medium-high heat.

Add the cardamom pods, cinnamon stick and bay leaves to cook for 2 minutes.

Reduce the heat to medium and add the onion along with a big pinch of salt.

Fry for 6-8 minutes until softened, then stir in the grated garlic and ginger along with the cumin, coriander and turmeric.

Fry the spices for 2 minutes, then add the lamb mince and fry for a further 10 minutes, stirring regularly, until it begins to colour.

Stir in the tinned tomatoes and 100ml of water, turn the heat down to a low simmer, cover with a lid and leave to cook for 20-25 minutes.

FOR THE ROTI

Divide the rested dough into 8 balls, then lightly oil each one and cover with a damp tea towel. One at a time, roll the balls into 20cm circles. Place a frying pan over a high heat and have the remaining ghee, a brush and a clean tea towel ready.

Place a roti into the hot pan and cook for 2 minutes, until the top is starting to look a little dry, then flip over. Brush with the melted ghee, cook for 2 minutes, then flip back over and brush with a little more ghee so both sides are coated.

Cook the roti for a couple more minutes, until charred spots have appeared on the surface. Wrap in the clean tea towel while you cook the remaining dough.

TO SERVE

Once the keema and roti are cooked, turn the heat back up under the keema pan and stir in the frozen peas and garam masala.

Cook for 2 minutes until the peas are bright green, then season with salt and pepper.

Top the keema with the sliced green chilli and serve it with the yoghurt and hot rotis.

JERK CHICKEN SKEWERS WITH COCONUT RICE

PREPARATION TIME: 30-45 MINUTES, PLUS 2-12 HOURS MARINATING | COOKING TIME: 20 MINUTES | SERVES 4

INGREDIENTS

4 chicken breasts, cut into 3cm chunks
2 red peppers, deseeded
2 yellow peppers, deseeded
Salt and pepper

FOR THE MARINADE

3 spring onions, chopped
2 cloves of garlic, peeled and quartered
2 scotch bonnets, quartered
2 tbsp olive oil
1 tbsp cider vinegar
1 tbsp soft brown sugar
1 tbsp thyme leaves
2 tsp ground allspice
2 tsp ground black pepper
1 tsp ground cinnamon
1 tsp chilli powder

FOR THE PINEAPPLE SALSA

350g fresh pineapple, finely chopped
25g fresh coriander, finely chopped
1 red onion, finely chopped
1 lime

FOR THE RICE

250g basmati rice
400ml tinned coconut milk

METHOD

FOR THE MARINADE

Start by blitzing all the ingredients together in a food processor until you have a paste.

Place the chicken into a large bowl, add the marinade and rub all over, using gloves as the marinade is spicy!

Cover with cling film and place in the fridge for at least 2 hours, preferably overnight.

Next, submerge 8 wooden skewers in cold water and leave to soak for 30 minutes.

FOR THE PINEAPPLE SALSA

Mix all the ingredients together, first zesting the lime into the bowl, then squeezing over the juice. Season well and set aside.

FOR THE CHICKEN SKEWERS

Thread the marinated chicken pieces onto the soaked skewers, alternating the meat with chunks of red and yellow pepper.

Lay on a foil-lined baking sheet and set the grill to a high heat.

Rinse the rice in a sieve until the water runs clear, then pour into a pan with the coconut milk, 120ml of fresh water and a big pinch of salt.

Bring to the boil, then reduce to a simmer, cover with a lid and cook for 10 minutes. Remove from the heat and take off the lid but don't touch the rice! Cover with a clean tea towel, replace the lid over the tea towel, and leave to steam for 10-12 minutes.

While the rice steams, brush the jerk chicken skewers with olive oil, season with a little salt and then slide them under the hot grill.

Cook for 10-12 minutes, turning regularly, until charred in places and cooked though.

TO SERVE

Spoon the coconut rice onto plates, top with the chicken skewers and serve with the pineapple salsa.

> Stay calm and let things be; don't get stressed over things you can't control. Personally, I go to the gym and practice Stoicism to look after my mental health.
>
> TROY VON SCHEIBNER (@TROYMAGICIAN)

MEXICAN CHICKEN & LIME TORTILLA SOUP

PREPARATION TIME: 30-45 MINUTES | COOKING TIME: 2 HOURS 10 MINUTES | SERVES 4

INGREDIENTS

FOR THE SOUP

1 whole chicken (approx. 1.5kg)

1 onion, chopped

1 stick of celery, chopped

1 ancho chilli, deseeded

1 tsp allspice berries

2 tbsp olive oil

2 large tomatoes, chopped

4 cloves of garlic, minced

1 jalapeño chilli, chopped

1 tsp salt

230g cooked black beans, drained

3 limes, juiced

FOR THE TOTOPOS

1 litre sunflower oil

4 corn tortillas, cut into strips

TO SERVE

1 avocado, diced

50g grated cotija or feta cheese, crumbled

METHOD

FOR THE SOUP

Put the chicken, onion, celery, ancho chilli and allspice into a large pot.

Cover with water and bring to the boil, then reduce to a simmer and cook for 1 hour with the lid off.

Turn the heat off and allow the chicken to sit in the liquid for 20 minutes before removing and leaving to cool for 20-30 minutes.

Now, take all the meat off the carcass, shredding it gently, and set aside.

Strain the chicken cooking stock into a clean pan, bring to a simmer and reduce to 1 litre. Meanwhile, heat the oil in a large frying pan and fry the tomatoes, garlic and chilli with the salt until soft but not coloured.

Add this mixture to the reduced stock and simmer for 20 minutes.

Allow to cool a little before blending until smooth.

Stir the black beans and lime juice into the soup and season to taste.

FOR THE TOTOPOS

Heat the oil in a large pan (no more than two thirds full) to 190°c.

Fry the tortilla strips for 30 seconds or until crisp.

Drain on kitchen paper and sprinkle with a little salt so they stay crisp.

TO SERVE

Serve the soup in bowls topped with the shredded chicken, totopos, diced avocado and cotija or feta cheese. You can also scatter over some fresh coriander and extra sliced jalapeño chillies, if you like.

> I work out often and have regular sessions with my therapist to look after my own mental health. My advice to others would be follow your creativity and don't suffer in silence.
>
> JIM CHAPMAN (@JIMCHAPMAN)

AROUND THE TABLE
– WITH –
ALEXINA GRAHAM

A LITTLE ABOUT ME

I'm a fashion model currently living in NYC and a proud Beder ambassador. My own journey with mental health started close to home, when towards the end of 2019, my sister told me that she didn't want to be here anymore, after many years of struggling with her mental health. Fortunately, we were able to intervene in time and we admitted her to a mental health hospital, where she stayed for six weeks. Since then, I have been working towards breaking the stigma around mental health and suicide alongside my professional career.

MENTAL HEALTH AND FASHION

The world of fashion doesn't often acknowledge the issues surrounding mental health and the importance of those conversations. Models can be seriously impacted by the ups and downs that come with the fashion industry, as we don't usually have control over our day-to-day life, which can be very stressful. I took the initiative to start a clothing brand, Xina, which combines fashion and mental health awareness with 5% of each sale going to Beder in the UK and Crisis Text Line in the US.

LOOKING AFTER MYSELF

From the moment you join the modelling industry, you're on your own and that can be very scary. We have to grow up quickly and fend for ourselves. These experiences have made me the adult I am today, so I wouldn't change anything. The tough times have made me stronger but finding things I enjoy doing outside of modelling has been crucial to my mental health. Personally, I have to go for a walk or do something outside to get my endorphins going, which changes my mood straight away. Getting the body moving, turning the phone or laptop off, and getting outdoors really has a positive impact on my mental health. I've also learnt when to take a break from social media, and now I only follow positive quotes, affirmations, and mental health content with everything else muted. It's about not putting too much pressure on yourself and avoiding all that comparison.

MY SUPPORT NETWORK

When I'm struggling personally, I turn to my mum and sister. My sister has been through the ups and downs of depression, so she understands me when I talk to her about how I'm feeling. My mum always reminds me of everything that's good in my life which helps too. I always say "take time to check in on your family and friends, or even strangers, and maybe you can help them by showing them love, compassion and kindness."

CHICKEN & CARAMELISED LEEK PIE

PREPARATION TIME: 15 MINUTES | COOKING TIME: 1 HOUR 45 MINUTES | SERVES 6

INGREDIENTS

FOR THE FILLING

1 tbsp olive oil

2 leeks, finely sliced

Salt and black pepper

8 skinless and boneless chicken thighs, cut into pieces

25g plain flour, seasoned

250g button mushrooms

200ml white wine

1 clove of garlic, minced

½ tsp finely chopped rosemary

300ml chicken stock

300ml double cream

1 tbsp chopped parsley

FOR THE PASTRY

2 packs of ready-rolled puff pastry

1 egg yolk, whisked

TO SERVE

Green vegetables

METHOD

FOR THE FILLING

Heat the olive oil in a large sauté pan.

Add the leeks and a pinch of salt, reduce the heat and cover with a lid.

Cook slowly for 20-30 minutes until soft, sweet and caramelised. Set aside.

Coat the chicken pieces with the seasoned flour, then brown in batches using the sauté pan, adding more oil as necessary.

Transfer to a bowl.

Cook the mushrooms in the same pan until they have released some moisture and are beginning to caramelise.

Add the white wine, stir to deglaze the pan and simmer until most of the liquid has gone.

Add the garlic, rosemary, chicken stock and cream, then reduce the heat.

Add the leeks and chicken back to the pan and simmer, uncovered, for 30 minutes or until the chicken is cooked through.

Stir in the parsley and season the filling to taste.

FOR THE PASTRY

Preheat the oven to 200°c/180°c fan/Gas Mark 6.

Unroll the puff pastry and cut off a strip that will fit around the rim of your pie dish.

Brush the dish with egg yolk to stick down the strip. From the remaining pastry, cut out strips for a lattice.

Add the filling to the pie dish and lattice the pastry on top, ensuring you leave a gap for steam. Brush with egg yolk and pop into the fridge for 15 minutes.

Brush the pie with egg yolk again and bake in the preheated oven for 20-30 minutes, or until the pastry is golden brown and the filling is bubbling.

TO SERVE

Rest for 5 minutes before serving with green vegetables.

Don't put too much pressure on yourself and avoid comparisons with others; exercising doesn't have to mean a full workout. Even a 5 minute walk helps, and you might find that it turns into something more because you start feeling good once you're out there.

ALEXINA GRAHAM (@ALEXINAGRAHAM)

LOBSTER MAC 'N' CHEESE

PREPARATION TIME: 15-30 MINUTES | COOKING TIME: 1 HOUR 5 MINUTES | SERVES 4

INGREDIENTS

1 cooked lobster (approx. 500g)

1 tbsp olive oil

1 large onion, finely chopped

Salt and pepper

50g butter

2 cloves of garlic, finely chopped

1 tbsp tomato purée

1 tsp smoked paprika

125ml white wine

50g flour

1 litre whole milk

1 tsp Dijon mustard

80g cheddar cheese, grated

80g gruyère cheese, grated

400g macaroni

50g parmesan

METHOD

Twist the claws off the lobster, then bash with a rolling pin to crack them open, pick out the meat and set aside. Peel the tail to reveal the fleshy meat.

Roughly chop the lobster meat, then place in a covered bowl in the fridge.

Heat the olive oil in a wide shallow casserole dish over a medium-high heat, then add the onion and a large pinch of salt. If you don't have a casserole dish, use a large saucepan and then tip the finished mac 'n' cheese mixture into an ovenproof dish to go in the oven.

Fry the onion for 3-5 minutes until softening, then add the butter.

Once it has melted, add the garlic, tomato purée and smoked paprika to fry for 2 minutes.

Pour in the wine and let it reduce until the liquid has almost disappeared.

Stir in the flour and cook for a couple of minutes.

Whisking continuously, add the milk to the pan a little at a time, allowing each addition to be fully absorbed before the next goes in.

Once you have added all the milk, whisk in the mustard and let the sauce bubble away for 5 minutes.

Add the cheddar and gruyère, stir to combine, season with salt and pepper if needed, then set aside.

Bring a large pan of salted water to the boil and preheat the oven to 190°c/170°c fan/ Gas Mark 5. Cook the pasta according to the instructions on the packet, then use a slotted spoon to transfer the macaroni into the pan of sauce.

Stir the mixture well, adding some of the pasta water to loosen the sauce a little.

Fold in the prepared lobster meat, smooth out the mixture or tip into a dish as required, then finely grate the parmesan over the top.

Bake the mac 'n' cheese in the preheated oven for 30-35 minutes, until golden and bubbling. Allow to cool for 10 minutes before serving.

"

Having friends that I can talk to about anything is the most important thing for my mental health.
Go easy on yourself and learn to love yourself more than anything else.

JAY MORTON (@JAY_MORTON)

ONE-PAN TIKKA ROAST CHICKEN

PREPARATION TIME: 10-25 MINUTES | COOKING TIME: 1 HOUR-1 HOUR 20 MINUTES | SERVES 4

INGREDIENTS

1.4-1.5kg free-range whole chicken, removed from the fridge 30-60 minutes before cooking

3 tbsp tikka curry paste

750g baby potatoes

2 onions

2 tsp cumin seeds

2 tsp ground coriander

1 tsp ground turmeric

Sea salt and black pepper

Vegetable, sunflower or olive oil

2 peppers (red, green or both), cut into roughly 3cm chunks

1 red chilli, finely sliced

½ lemon

Handful of coriander leaves

TO SERVE

Plain yoghurt

Mango chutney

Steamed basmati rice or naan bread

METHOD

Preheat the oven to 200°c/180°c fan/Gas Mark 6.

Rub the chicken all over with the tikka paste, making sure it's thoroughly coated, then set aside while you prep the vegetables.

Chop the potatoes into chunks and quarter the onions.

Place the potatoes and onions in a large roasting tray.

Sprinkle over the cumin, coriander, turmeric, two big pinches of salt and a grind of black pepper, then toss until coated. Drizzle in oil and toss again.

Place the tikka chicken on top of the potatoes and onions, drizzle with oil and sprinkle over some sea salt.

Place on the middle shelf of the preheated oven for between 1 hour and 1 hour 20 minutes (depending on the size of the chicken) or until cooked through. To test this, stick a knife into the thickest part of the thigh and make sure the juices run clear and/or use a meat thermometer, which should read at least 75°c.

When the chicken is halfway through its cooking time, remove the tray from the oven and move the potatoes and onions around with a spatula, then add the peppers and half the sliced red chilli before placing it back in the oven.

Once the chicken is cooked, remove the tray from the oven and leave to rest for 5 minutes before serving. Taste and season, if necessary, then squeeze over the juice of half a lemon and scatter with the remaining red chilli and a handful of coriander leaves.

All the spiced meat juices will have collected at the bottom of the pan, so use a spoon to drizzle these over the chicken once served.

Serve with rice or naan. Plain yoghurt and mango chutney are also nice additions.

MIDDLE EASTERN SLOW-COOKED LAMB

PREPARATION TIME: 2-24 HOURS | COOKING TIME: 3 HOURS 30 MINUTES | SERVES 2-4

INGREDIENTS

1 tsp ground coriander

2 tbsp baharat spice blend

2 tbsp olive oil

1½ lemons

Sea salt and black pepper

1-1.2kg bone-in lamb shoulder

2 cloves of garlic, sliced

2 small red onions, quartered

2 handfuls of pomegranate seeds

Handful of fresh herbs (parsley and/or mint work well)

METHOD

In a bowl, mix the spices and olive oil with the zest and juice of 1 lemon.

Add some black pepper and a generous pinch or two of sea salt, then whisk together to make a marinade.

Make around 10-15 small slits across the surface of the lamb with a small knife, then push a slice of garlic into each one.

Put the lamb in a roasting tray (big enough to fit the lamb and onions in) and rub all over with the marinade until the whole shoulder is covered.

Cover with foil and leave to marinate in the fridge for at least 2 hours, preferably overnight.

Before cooking, let the lamb come to room temperature and preheat the oven to 150°c/130°c fan/Gas Mark 2.

Add 100ml of water and the quartered onions to the roasting tray, then re-seal the whole tray with foil.

Roast in the oven for 3 hours, checking every hour and basting the lamb with the juices. If the liquid dries out, add a splash more water.

Once the lamb is cooked, remove from the oven, cover and allow to rest for 30 minutes.

TO SERVE

Shred the lamb using two forks.

Taste and season with salt, if necessary, then squeeze over the juice of half a lemon.

Use a spoon to drizzle the juices from the roasting tray over the meat, then scatter over the pomegranate seeds and fresh herbs.

Serve the lamb with flatbreads, accompanied by yoghurt, herbs and pickles.

Exercise and sport are my main tools for looking after my mental health, closely followed by any other activities that distract me from thinking too much. Cooking has always been a passion, but Birch has also helped reignite some other pastimes such as pottery and gardening which I find fulfilling, especially when shared with my kids.

CHRIS KING (@CKROAMING)

STAY TRUE TO WHO YOU ARE AND DON'T
WORRY IF OTHERS DON'T LIKE THAT.
YOU'RE NOT HERE FOR EVERYONE,
SO DON'T LOSE YOURSELF JUST BECAUSE
SOMEONE ELSE MIGHT NOT LIKE IT.

BEN BIDWELL

JAMAICAN OXTAIL STEW WITH CRISPY POTATOES

PREPARATION TIME: 30-45 MINUTES, PLUS OVERNIGHT MARINATING | COOKING TIME: 3 HOURS 30 MINUTES | SERVES 6

INGREDIENTS

1kg oxtail

3 tsp Caribbean curry powder or hot curry powder

2 tbsp Worcestershire sauce

1 tbsp soy sauce

1 tsp browning (such as Maggi)

1 tbsp brown sugar

1 tsp garlic granules

1 tsp onion granules

2 tbsp vegetable oil

2 onions, roughly chopped

4 cloves of garlic, minced

700-800ml beef stock

10g fresh thyme

5g fresh rosemary

2 bay leaves

1 sweet potato, cut into 3cm cubes

½ butternut squash, cut into 3cm cubes

2 corn on the cob, cut into pieces

1 red pepper, cut into chunks

2 tbsp butter

Salt, to season

FOR THE CRISPY POTATOES

24 new potatoes, scrubbed but unpeeled

3 tbsp olive oil

METHOD

Mix the oxtail with the curry powder, Worcestershire sauce, soy sauce, browning, sugar, and garlic and onion granules in a large non-reactive bowl.

Place the bowl into the fridge for at least 4 hours, but ideally overnight.

Take the bowl out of the fridge and allow the mixture to come to room temperature.

Pour the vegetable oil into a large pan over a medium-high heat, then brown the meat for about 3 minutes on each side in batches. Place the browned meat in a bowl and set aside.

Add the onions to the pan and cook for 3-4 minutes, stirring until golden and covered in the delicious spice. Add the garlic and cook for 1 more minute.

Deglaze the pan with a little of the stock, scraping up the crispy bits from the base of the pan to incorporate the flavour.

Put the oxtail back into the pan, along with any juices, then add the remaining stock and herbs. Bring to the boil and then reduce to a simmer.

Simmer the stew for 2 hours, covered with a lid.

After this time, add the sweet potato, squash, corn cobs and red pepper.

Cook the stew for a further hour, or until the meat is falling off the bone.

FOR THE CRISPY POTATOES

Preheat the oven to 180°c/160°c fan/Gas Mark 4.

Boil the potatoes for 8 minutes in salted water.

Drain and allow to steam dry, then arrange the potatoes on a baking sheet and lightly crush with a fork.

Drizzle with the oil and bake for 20-25 minutes, or until crisp.

Remove the lid from the stew, taste and add some butter and salt, if needed. If the gravy is a little thin, strain the liquid into a pan and heat until reduced slightly.

Serve the meat and vegetables with the gravy and potatoes.

Exercise is key to looking after my mental health – boxing, bike rides, going to the gym – along with not getting involved with the small stuff. Keep a bird's eye view over everything is the advice I would give to my younger self.

JOHNNY NELSON (@JOHNNYNELSONSKY)

FUNDAMENTAL PRINCIPLES

I was a super sensitive kid and struggled to enjoy school for various reasons which led to behaviour that eventually got me expelled. I started hanging out with a group of boys who were dabbling in drugs and things quickly spiralled out of control for me. At the age of 21, with the amazing support of my parents, I got into a Christian rehabilitation centre in South Africa and spent about 8 months there. It completely changed my life because I really understood how lost I was as an individual and how deep-rooted my addiction was. The religion itself didn't click with me but what it did give me was a set of fundamental principles to live by – basic things like being nice to other people, not harbouring resentment, saying sorry when you're in the wrong – which have held me in such good stead throughout my journey with mental wellbeing.

THE POWER OF PIZZA

The real work began when I left the treatment centre. I was so fiercely determined not to allow my sobriety to make me socially isolated that I let my friends drink around me, but it was killing me – I felt so vulnerable, so isolated, so lonely. I had to find a different way to socialise in a safe environment, so I threw myself into cooking. One evening I made pizzas using a conventional oven, which turned out soggy and a bit rubbish, but I loved the process of it. I decided to build a proper pizza oven in the garden, even though my girlfriend Laura – who's now my wife – said I was crazy and we really didn't have the money, but I did it and suddenly my friends stopped bringing beers and started bringing pizza toppings. My garden became a safe haven for me, and I knew I had to build a business that brought this sense of community to other people in their own homes too. That was the starting point of Gozney and I set out on a mission to make live-fire cooking accessible for all.

MAINTAINING BALANCE

As a recovering addict, I can easily end up channelling all my energy into one facet of my life. Even though I'm now 15 years sober, it's very easy for me to cross-addict into overworking, overeating or training too much. I work really hard to find and maintain balance between work, spending time with my family and nurturing my own physical and mental wellbeing. One of the ways that I disempower negative experiences when I can feel my mental health becoming more vulnerable is talking about how I'm feeling. There's such stigma around needing to 'man up and get on with it' and I think so many people feel like they're not allowed to open up and share their feelings but our own mental health is so unique and there's absolutely nothing to be ashamed about if you're not coping.

SPICED LAMB PIZZA

PREPARATION TIME: 24 HOURS | COOKING TIME: 5 MINUTES | MAKES 3

INGREDIENTS

FOR THE 24-HOUR DOUGH
310g water
0.1g dry yeast
13g salt
500g 00 tipo flour or strong white bread flour

FOR THE SPICED LAMB
200g ground lamb
1 tsp ground coriander
1 tsp ground cumin
1 tsp chopped fresh parsley
1 tsp chopped fresh mint
1 ½ tsp chopped toasted pine nuts

FOR THE TOMATO SAUCE
1 tin of tomatoes
½ onion, diced
2 cloves of garlic, sliced
1 red chilli, chopped
1 tbsp each mint sauce, tomato ketchup and white wine vinegar

FOR THE DUKKHA
1 tbsp each blanched hazelnuts and sesame seeds
1 tbsp cumin seeds
½ tbsp pistachios
½ tbsp coriander seeds
1 tsp salt

FOR EACH PIZZA
1 dough ball
45g each mozzarella cheese, spiced lamb and tomato sauce
1 tbsp each yoghurt, dukkha and chopped fresh mint/parsley

METHOD

FOR THE 24-HOUR DOUGH

Pour the water into a bowl and add the yeast, then whisk to break apart.

Combine the salt and flour, then begin adding them to the liquid, mixing continuously with your hand. Once mixed, knead the dough for 5-6 minutes.

Shape into a ball, cover with a clean bowl and leave to rest for 20 minutes.

Knead the rested dough again for a final minute or two before reshaping into a ball. Place into a container, cover and leave to ferment at room temperature for 16 hours.

Place the dough on a clean, flourless surface and divide into three 270g pieces.

Shape these into dough balls and then place on a tray, cover and refrigerate for at least 4 and no more than 10 hours.

Remove the dough balls from the fridge 3-5 hours before you want to bake the pizzas, allowing the gluten to relax. Then simply toss the room temperature dough ball into a tub of flour, shake off the excess, and open into a pizza base.

FOR THE SPICED LAMB

Combine all the ingredients for the spiced lamb by hand in a bowl, then season with salt and pepper. Cover and refrigerate until required.

FOR THE TOMATO SAUCE

Put all the tomato sauce ingredients in a blender and pulse until you reach the desired consistency. Taste to check the seasoning, cover and set aside.

FOR THE DUKKHA

Place all the ingredients for the dukkha into a pestle and mortar, bash into a slightly rough crumb consistency, then set aside.

TO MAKE THE PIZZA

Top your pizza base with the mozzarella cheese, add small pieces of the spiced lamb mixture and spoon over the tomato sauce in a swirl.

For best results, use an outdoor pizza oven. Bake the pizza for 90 seconds, rotating part-way through. If you are using a standard indoor oven, simply crank the temperature up high and leave it to heat up for at least 30 minutes before you want to cook. Ensure the tray you plan to place your pizza on is preheated.

Finish the cooked pizza with a blob of yoghurt, a sprinkle of dukkha and the fresh herbs.

SUKKA LAMB CURRY

PREPARATION TIME: 10-25 MINUTES | COOKING TIME: 2 HOURS 20 MINUTES | SERVES 4

INGREDIENTS

3 tbsp ghee

1 bay leaf

1 cinnamon stick

4 cardamon pods

2 onions, sliced

5 cloves of garlic, peeled

15g (thumb-sized piece) fresh ginger, peeled and roughly chopped

800g diced lamb

3 large tomatoes (350g)

3 cloves

2 tsp mustard seeds

2 tsp cumin seeds

2 tsp ground coriander

2 tsp garam masala

1 tsp ground turmeric

1 tsp red chilli powder

25g fresh coriander, roughly chopped

Salt and pepper

METHOD

Melt the ghee in a large saucepan over a medium heat.

Once melted, add the bay leaf, cinnamon stick and cardamon pods to toast for a minute until fragrant.

Add the sliced onions along with a big pinch of salt and fry for 10 minutes, until the onions are softened.

Blitz the garlic and ginger to a chunky paste, then add this to the pan and fry for a minute. Increase the heat to medium-high, then add the diced lamb and cook for 5-7 minutes until evenly coloured.

Using the same blender or food processor, blitz the tomatoes to a purée and set aside.

Stir the cloves, mustard seeds, cumin seeds and ground coriander into the lamb mixture and cook for 2 minutes.

Add the blitzed tomatoes to the pan along with 250ml of water, then turn the heat right down to a simmer.

Cover with a lid and cook the curry for between 1 hour 50 minutes and 2 hours, stirring occasionally, until the lamb chunks are tender.

Remove the lid and turn the heat back up to medium-high.

Stir in the garam masala, turmeric and chilli powder, then cook for 1-2 minutes until the sauce is coating the lamb.

TO SERVE

Add most of the chopped coriander, stir well and season to taste with salt and pepper. Serve the curry with rice or naan, topped with the remaining fresh coriander.

> Mental health is vital to us all and we all need to look out for each other. When feeling low, I call my friends and move my body: walking, swimming, yoga, golf and meditation all help. I also love trying new recipes; making food for someone who enjoys it is such a pleasure and cooking is a time to slow down and be mindful.
> DI STEWART (@DISTEWART79)

PULLED PORK TOSTADAS

PREPARATION TIME: 25-40 MINUTES | COOKING TIME: 2 HOURS 40 MINUTES | SERVES 4-6

INGREDIENTS

FOR THE PULLED PORK

1 tbsp olive oil

2 tsp paprika

2 tsp brown sugar

800g boneless pork shoulder joint

250ml boiling vegetable stock

80g BBQ sauce

Sea salt

FOR THE SALSA

3 large tomatoes, diced

1 red onion, finely chopped

1 lime, zested and juiced

1 chilli, finely chopped

Handful of fresh coriander, chopped

TO SERVE

8-10 small tortillas

2 corn on the cob

1 tsp olive oil

100g cheddar, grated

Handful of fresh coriander leaves

METHOD

FOR THE PULLED PORK

Preheat the oven to 160°c/140°c fan/Gas Mark 3.

Combine the oil, paprika and brown sugar and brush this mixture over the pork.

Heat a large frying pan, then put the pork in the pan and sear on each side until golden.

Transfer the pork to a roasting tin or casserole dish with a lid, skin side up.

Pour the stock into the bottom of the roasting tin and season the pork with salt.

Cover the tin tightly with foil or put the lid of the dish on and cook for 2 hours to 2 hours 20 minutes until it's nearly falling apart, turning over halfway through.

Transfer the pork into a bowl and leave to rest for 10 minutes.

Take 4 tablespoons of the liquid left in the roasting dish and mix it with the BBQ sauce. Cut the skin off and then shred the pork into a bowl using two forks.

Coat the pork with the barbecue mixture.

For the tostada shells, turn the oven temperature up to 220°c/200°c fan/Gas Mark 7 and place the tortillas in a single layer on 2 baking trays.

Brush both sides lightly with oil and to stop them from curling in the oven, place a wire rack upside down on top of them. Bake for 6-8 minutes until golden and crisp.

FOR THE SALSA

Toss all the salsa ingredients together with a pinch of salt and set aside.

TO SERVE

Parboil the corn cobs for 5 minutes, drain and brush with olive oil.

Griddle the cobs for 5-10 minutes, turning regularly, until the corn has charred all over. Slice the corn off the cob with a sharp knife.

Load the crispy tostada shells with the barbecue pulled pork, salsa, charred corn, grated cheddar and fresh coriander leaves.

> My advice to anyone would be embrace yourself. We are taught from an early age by society that we need to be funnier, smarter, richer, more athletic, popular and that any part of your personality that doesn't fit with this status quo needs to be blunted or hidden to 'fit in'. Find your lane, find what makes you happy and content, and own it.
>
> KRIS HALL

CHAPTER

5

SWEET TREATS

This chapter contains scrumptious desserts and a range of baking recipes for every occasion to satisfy your sweet tooth.

OAT CHOCOLATE CHIP MUFFINS

PREPARATION TIME: 20-35 MINUTES | COOKING TIME: 40 MINUTES | MAKES 12-14

INGREDIENTS

FOR THE MUFFINS

125g unsalted butter

125g soft dark brown sugar

2 eggs

150ml natural yoghurt

1 tsp baking powder

175g self-raising flour

50g rolled oats

100g dark chocolate, roughly chopped

FOR THE CRUMBLE TOPPING

40g rolled oats

35g self-raising flour

35g soft dark brown sugar

35g cold unsalted butter, cubed

35g dark chocolate, roughly chopped

METHOD

FOR THE MUFFINS

Preheat the oven to 180°c/160°c fan/Gas Mark 4.

Beat the butter and sugar together using an electric whisk or stand mixer for 3-4 minutes until light and fluffy.

Scrape down the sides with a spatula and gradually whisk in the eggs, one at a time, and then the yoghurt until combined.

Fold in the baking powder, flour, oats and chocolate until everything is just combined and there are no pockets of flour left.

Line a 12-hole muffin tin with muffin cases and fill each case with the mixture so it's three quarters full.

FOR THE CRUMBLE TOPPING

Put all the ingredients into a bowl and rub with your fingertips until you have a crumble-like texture. Some of the mixture should hold together in clumps.

Sprinkle the topping over the muffin mixture in the cases.

Bake the crumble-topped muffins for 35-40 minutes until they are golden brown and a skewer inserted in the centre comes out clean.

Take them out of the oven and cool on a wire rack before serving or storing.

> Pay attention to your mental health and don't be afraid to stand out by doing so.
> Things that help me look after myself include walking my dogs, getting fresh air and spending time with family and friends. Self-reflection can also be useful, alongside activities I really enjoy like cooking.
> MILLIE BRIGHT (@MBRIGHTY04)

DATE & SALTED CARAMEL CAKE

PREPARATION TIME: 35-50 MINUTES, PLUS 30 MINUTES CHILLING | COOKING TIME: 40 MINUTES | SERVES 12

INGREDIENTS

FOR THE SPONGE

175g pitted dates, roughly chopped

1 tsp bicarbonate of soda

225g softened unsalted butter, plus extra for greasing

100g dark brown sugar

100g caster sugar

3 eggs

300g self-raising flour

FOR THE ICING

150g softened unsalted butter

350g icing sugar

250g tinned caramel

1 ½ tbsp milk

Sea salt flakes

METHOD

FOR THE SPONGE

Preheat the oven to 180°c/160°c fan/Gas Mark 4.

Grease and line two 18cm sandwich tins with butter and parchment paper.

Put the dates, bicarbonate of soda and 200ml of boiling water into a bowl, cover and leave to sit for 15 minutes.

Meanwhile, beat the butter and both types of sugar together with an electric whisk or using a stand mixer for 3-4 minutes until light and fluffy. Scrape down the sides using a spatula and gradually beat in the eggs one at a time, then fold in the flour.

Using a hand whisk, whisk the soaked dates into the water so you have a purée. Fold this into the cake mixture so it's all combined.

Divide between the two tins and bake in the preheated oven for 35-40 minutes until golden and a skewer inserted comes out clean.

Remove the cakes from the tins and leave to cool on a wire rack.

FOR THE ICING

Beat the butter and icing sugar with 100g of the caramel in a large bowl with an electric whisk until light, pale and fluffy.

Whisk the milk into the icing, then spoon into a piping bag with a large round nozzle.

Beat the remaining caramel with a pinch of sea salt to make the drizzle.

Place one of the sponges on a cake board or plate.

Pipe the icing on top in blobs all the way around the sides and in the middle too.

Drizzle or pipe the salted caramel into the gaps, then put the cake in the fridge for 30 minutes to slightly set the icing.

Place the other sponge on top of the chilled icing.

Continue piping the remaining icing on top of the sponge in blobs.

Drizzle or pipe the remaining caramel in between the icing to finish.

Don't be afraid to share how you're feeling with those around you.
It's better to talk about something that's upsetting you than to keep it to yourself.

PRIYA GOPALDAS (@PRIYAGOPALDAS)

APPLE CRUMBLE PIE

PREPARATION TIME: 35-50 MINUTES, PLUS CHILLING TIME | COOKING TIME: 1 HOUR 5 MINUTES | SERVES 8-10

INGREDIENTS

FOR THE PASTRY

200g plain flour

100g cold unsalted butter, cubed

50g icing sugar

Pinch of salt

1 large egg yolk

FOR THE FILLING

600g cooking apples

½ tbsp vanilla extract

1 tbsp ground cinnamon

50g caster sugar

50g light brown sugar

FOR THE CRUMBLE

135g plain flour

85g cold unsalted butter, cubed

35g rolled oats

25g caster sugar

25g light brown sugar

½ tsp ground cinnamon

METHOD

FOR THE PASTRY

In a bowl, rub the flour and butter together until the mixture looks like breadcrumbs.

Stir in the sugar and salt, followed by the egg yolk, and bring it together. Add 1-2 tablespoons of cold water to form a soft dough. Tip out on a clean surface and form into a ball, kneading lightly until smooth.

Roll out the pastry between two sheets of baking paper into a circle of around 30cm.

If it's too soft to handle, chill the pastry for around 30 minutes until slightly firmer.

Lay the pastry into a 23cm tart tin or pie dish, pushing gently into the corners, then trim the edges so there's around 1cm of pastry overhanging the rim. Prick the pastry base several times with a fork, then chill for 45 minutes.

Preheat the oven to 200°c/180°c fan/Gas Mark 6.

Scrunch up a piece of parchment large enough to cover the tart tin, then un-scrunch, and place on top of the chilled pastry. Fill the pastry case to the top with baking beans or uncooked rice. Bake in the preheated oven for 15 minutes, then remove the beans and parchment and bake for 10-15 more minutes until the pastry is golden brown.

Leave to cool in the tin, then trim off the excess pastry around the rim.

FOR THE FILLING

Turn the oven down to 180°c/160°c fan/Gas Mark 4.

Peel and core the apples, then cut into 1-2cm chunks. Toss the apples with the vanilla, cinnamon, both sugars, and a pinch of salt before putting them into the pastry case.

FOR THE CRUMBLE

Rub the flour into the butter with your fingertips to create a rough breadcrumb-like mixture. Stir through the oats, both sugars and cinnamon. Sprinkle the crumble topping over the apple filling and bake the pie in the oven for 40-45 minutes, or until the topping is lightly golden brown and the fruit beneath is cooked but still has a bit of bite.

Remove from the tin and serve warm with vanilla ice cream.

> I've loved cooking since I was young. I've always found it so relaxing and enjoyable, so it's definitely something that helps me look after my mental health. I also try to focus on small wins on a daily basis, little things that keep me happy and add up to a positive outlook. If I could talk to my younger self though, I would say to not get too wrapped up in negative situations and also to try and find the right ways and people to communicate with.

MARVIN SORDELL (@MARVINSORDELL)

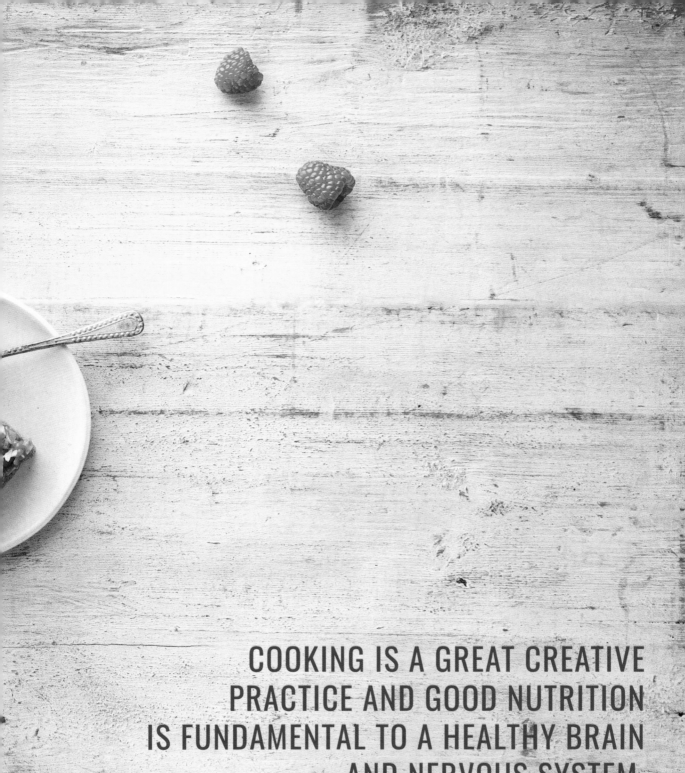

COOKING IS A GREAT CREATIVE
PRACTICE AND GOOD NUTRITION
IS FUNDAMENTAL TO A HEALTHY BRAIN
AND NERVOUS SYSTEM.

DALE PINNOCK

BARMBRACK

PREPARATION TIME: 15-30 MINUTES, PLUS OVERNIGHT SOAKING | COOKING TIME: 1 HOUR | SERVES 8-10

INGREDIENTS

2 black teabags

300g sultanas

50g mixed peel

1 orange, zested

75ml whiskey

75g caster sugar

75g dark brown sugar

250g self-raising flour

1 tsp baking powder

1 tsp ground cinnamon

1 egg, beaten

METHOD

Place the teabags into a large bowl and pour 200ml of boiling water over them.

Leave to brew for 5 minutes, then remove the teabags and add the sultanas, mixed peel, orange zest, whiskey and both sugars into the liquid.

Stir to combine and allow the sugar to dissolve.

Cover tightly and leave overnight at room temperature for all the liquid to be absorbed.

The next day, preheat the oven to 180°c/160°c fan/Gas Mark 4.

Grease and line a 900g (2lb) loaf tin with non-stick greaseproof paper.

Put the flour, baking powder and cinnamon into a large bowl and gradually fold in the soaked sultana mixture and the beaten egg, mixing until everything is combined and there are no lumps of flour left.

Pour the barmbrack mixture into the prepared tin and bake for 50 minutes to 1 hour until cooked through. Place a piece of foil over the top if it begins to brown too much. Leave to cool in the tin.

Once cool you can eat the barmbrack straightaway, sliced and slathered with butter.

"

Healthy food means a healthy mind. You are what you eat! I find my mood always improves when I eat good food. I always try to drink lots of water and work out; I work out in the gym and do Muay Thai kickboxing to look after my mental health.

DANNY O'DONOGHUE (@THESCRIPT_DANNY)

SALTED TAHINI BLONDIES

PREPARATION TIME: 15-30 MINUTES | COOKING TIME: 30 MINUTES | MAKES 15

INGREDIENTS

225g unsalted butter, melted, plus extra for greasing

200g light brown sugar

100g caster sugar

100g tahini

1 tsp fine sea salt

2 large eggs

1 egg yolk

2 tsp vanilla paste

250g plain flour

1 tsp baking powder

100g white chocolate, finely chopped

1 tsp sea salt flakes

½ tbsp sesame seeds

METHOD

Preheat the oven to 180°c/160°c fan/Gas Mark 4.

Grease and line a 30 by 20cm baking tin with butter and parchment paper.

Put the melted butter, both sugars, 50g of the tahini, and the fine salt into a mixing bowl and stir to combine.

Whisk the eggs, yolk and vanilla into the mixture until incorporated.

Fold the flour, baking powder and white chocolate into the blondie mixture until everything is combined, then pour into the prepared tin.

Beat the remaining tahini in a bowl to loosen and drizzle over the top of the mixture.

Swirl it in with a skewer or a spoon so it marbles with the batter, then top with the sea salt flakes and sesame seeds.

Bake the blondies for 25-30 minutes until golden brown so they are set around the outside and a little wobbly in the middle (this will set once cooled fully).

Allow the blondies to cool completely before slicing into a 3 by 5 grid to get 15 squares. If you're looking for perfect slices, you can even put the tin in the fridge overnight before cutting them.

"

There's nothing wrong with just enjoying what you have rather than always thinking you have to strive for better. Ambition can be toxic. People aren't going around judging you so relax about stuff!

FELICITY SPECTOR (@FELICITYSPECTOR)

GIOVANNA FLETCHER

MY MENTAL HEALTH JOURNEY

I've become more aware of my own mental health over the last few years but there have definitely been times throughout my teens and early twenties where it took a dip, so it did affect me at a much younger age than I realised at the time. Some of that was circumstantial; I was badly bullied as a kid and my way of dealing with that was to walk around the school field, making little stories up in my head and sometimes acting them out or singing. So, in a strange way, I feel like I wouldn't be doing what I am now if that hadn't happened.

HAPPY MUM, HAPPY BABY

For the last few years, my main focus has been on maternal mental health; a massive driving force behind my podcast (Happy Mum, Happy Baby) is the fact that the leading cause of death in new mums within the first year is suicide. That's why we do what we do, because we know that so many people feel like they're alone in experiencing those difficult feelings. Sometimes people come up to me and say that a particular episode has helped them or they really identified with something we talked about. Often it's quite emotional, which makes me realise how impactful it is to have those conversations out there, from the mundane to the very serious like postpartum psychosis. There are so many great books and podcasts on the subject now and I would really encourage anyone to take in what's available as well as talking to professionals or people in online communities that understand.

MENTAL HEALTH MATTERS

I've been someone who's said yes to everything for so long, without stopping to think about what's good for me. By the time I was able to say "it's too much" I had already reached breaking point, whereas now I'm more cautious and have more boundaries. There's more understanding now that sometimes people aren't coping. I think lockdown was actually part of that, from colleagues being humanised when we saw them in their homes over Zoom to checking in with friends more often. In my industry, from TV to the book world, it is a conversation that's happening more and more. I've always felt supported by my teams but it's in a very different way now and I don't feel as many people are scared to talk about their mental health.

STICKY TOFFEE CHEESECAKE PUDDING

PREPARATION TIME: 40-55 MINUTES | COOKING TIME: 45 MINUTES | SERVES 8-10

INGREDIENTS

FOR THE CHEESECAKE

200g full-fat cream cheese

100g mascarpone

75g caster sugar

1 tsp vanilla extract

1 large egg

FOR THE STICKY TOFFEE

175g Medjool dates, pitted (prepared weight)

100g butter, plus extra for greasing

125g light brown sugar

2 large eggs, beaten

200g plain flour

2 tsp baking powder

Pinch of salt

TO SERVE

100g Carnation caramel

Vanilla or salted caramel ice cream, to serve

Custard, to serve

METHOD

Preheat the oven to 180°c/160°c fan/Gas Mark 4.

Pour 275ml of boiling water over the pitted dates and leave to soak for 15 minutes.

Using a food processor, blitz until you have a smooth purée and then transfer into a bowl to cool.

FOR THE CHEESECAKE

Use an electric whisk or the paddle attachment on a stand mixer to beat the cream cheese, mascarpone, caster sugar and vanilla together for about 3-4 minutes until thickened. Don't worry if it seems runny to start with, as it will thicken again.

Scrape down the bowl using a spatula and then beat in the egg until combined.

FOR THE STICKY TOFFEE

Beat the butter and brown sugar together for 4-5 minutes using an electric whisk until light and fluffy, then scrape down the sides of the bowl and gradually add the beaten eggs until combined.

Tip in the flour, baking powder and salt, mix until everything is incorporated, then fold in the cooled date purée.

Spoon dots of the cheesecake mixture and dots of the sticky toffee mixture into a buttered baking dish and gently marble them with a skewer or a teaspoon.

Put the caramel into a small bowl and beat with a spoon to loosen, then drop tablespoons on top of the sticky toffee cheesecake and lightly marble them into the mix.

Bake the pudding for 45-50 minutes until a skewer inserted into the sticky toffee section comes out clean.

TO SERVE

Scoop the pudding into bowls and serve warm with ice cream or custard.

> Mental health is something we all need to focus on, especially with boys and men who are statistically more affected by suicide. As the mother of three young boys, it's something I think about for their future.
> My advice would be to keep checking in with your feelings and know that life is a collection of moments that pass. Sometimes those moments seem so huge and monumental it's hard to see past them, but they'll move on.
>
> GIOVANNA FLETCHER (@MRSGIFLETCHER)

CREAMY CACAO MOUSSE

PREPARATION TIME: 15-30 MINUTES, PLUS 4 HOURS SETTING | SERVES 4-6

INGREDIENTS

115g cashews

100g pitted dates

160ml almond milk

4 heaped tbsp cacao powder

1 tbsp coconut oil

Pinch of sea salt

TO SERVE

Raspberries

Strawberries

Coconut yoghurt

METHOD

Place the cashews into a bowl and cover with boiling water.

Leave to soak for at least 10 minutes to soften them before draining.

Once you have drained the cashews, place them into a powerful blender with the rest of the mousse ingredients and blend until everything comes together and the mixture turns smooth and creamy. This may take up to 10 minutes.

Taste the mixture to check the flavour; you can add more or less cacao powder depending on how rich and chocolatey you like your mousse and blend again, if needed.

Spoon the mixture into glasses or bowls and leave in the fridge to set for at least 4 hours.

TO SERVE

Finish the set mousse with your choice of topping: raspberries, strawberries or a big dollop of coconut yoghurt.

> There are four things that ground me: 1. Daily movement (a walk or some exercise). 2. Journaling (recording my gratitude and affirmations). 3. Eating and creating delicious recipes that are packed full of nutrient-dense ingredients. 4. Reducing screen time (especially when I first wake up or for the last hour of my day). These things combined have really helped to keep my mental health stable.
>
> STEPHANIE ELSWOOD (@STEPHELSWOOD)

MEXICAN HOT CHOCOLATE CAKE

PREPARATION TIME: 35-50 MINUTES | COOKING TIME: 30 MINUTES | SERVES 10-12

INGREDIENTS

FOR THE SPONGE

175g unsalted butter, plus extra for greasing

½ tbsp vanilla extract

3 large eggs

50ml milk

125g caster sugar

125g soft light brown sugar

250g self-raising flour

½ tsp baking powder

30g cocoa powder

1 tbsp ground cinnamon

½ tbsp ground ginger

½ tsp ground star anise

½ tsp cayenne pepper

Pinch of salt

FOR THE TOPPING

300ml double cream

75g soft light brown sugar

50g mini marshmallows

Dark chocolate, grated (optional)

Chilli flakes (optional)

METHOD

Preheat the oven to 180°c/160°c fan/Gas Mark 4.

Grease two 18cm sandwich cake tins with butter and line the bases with baking paper.

Cube the butter into a heatproof bowl and place in the microwave for 30 second bursts until melted.

Leave it to cool, then whisk in the vanilla, eggs and milk until combined.

Add the rest of the sponge ingredients to the butter mixture and stir until you have a smooth cake batter, making sure all the flour is combined.

Evenly divide the cake batter between the two prepared tins and bake in the preheated oven for 30 minutes, until a skewer inserted into the middle comes out clean.

Leave the cakes to cool in the tin for 30 minutes, then turn out onto a wire rack to cool.

In a large bowl, whisk the cream and brown sugar together until thick enough to just hold soft peaks.

Spread half of the cream on top of one cooled sponge, place the other sponge on top and spread the remaining cream on top of the cake.

TO SERVE

Sprinkle over the mini marshmallows and finish with some grated dark chocolate and chilli flakes, if you like.

> Cooking has definitely helped me look after my mental health. I think because it is a new challenge, and my mind is solely focused on making the dish the best I can, I don't think about anything else so can concentrate on something that makes me happy.
>
> RACHEL DALY (@RACHELDALY3)

CHOCOLATE & CHAMPAGNE TART

PREPARATION TIME: 50-65 MINUTES, PLUS SETTING | COOKING TIME: 25 MINUTES | SERVES 10

INGREDIENTS

FOR THE CHOCOLATE SABLÉ PASTRY

185g plain flour

80g icing sugar

50g cornflour

25g cocoa powder

1g salt

½ a vanilla pod, seeds scraped out

130g unsalted butter, at room temperature

1 large egg

FOR THE CHAMPAGNE GANACHE

100g champagne

25g water

10g cocoa powder, plus extra to dust

5 drops of rosewater

115g whipping cream

3 egg yolks

35g caster sugar

170g dark chocolate, roughly chopped

TO SERVE

Dried rose petals, to garnish

1 tin of peaches in syrup, drained

Fresh peach slices

Chantilly cream

METHOD

FOR THE CHOCOLATE SABLÉ PASTRY

Pulse the flour, icing sugar, cornflour, cocoa, and salt in a food processor until combined. Add the vanilla seeds and butter, pulse again until the texture is like coarse sand, then add the egg and pulse until the mixture only just forms a dough.

Form the pastry into a disc and wrap in cling film. Chill in the fridge for 45 minutes, along with a 22cm shallow tart ring greased with butter and placed on a baking tray lined with non-stick paper.

Preheat the oven to 170°c/150°c fan/Gas Mark 3 and lightly flour your work top. Quickly roll out the chilled pastry to the thickness of a £1 coin, about 2cm wider than your tart ring. Lay it inside the tart ring and gently coax into the edges, taking care not to stretch the pastry as this will cause it to shrink when cooking.

Trim off the excess with a sharp knife and chill for 10 minutes.

Prick the pastry base with a fork and line with baking paper. Fill the tart tin with baking beans or dry rice and bake in the preheated oven for 15 minutes, then uncover the pastry and bake for 5 more minutes. Leave to cool.

FOR THE CHAMPAGNE GANACHE

Whisk 25g of champagne with water, cocoa powder and rosewater to a smooth paste.

Combine this paste with the remaining champagne and cream, then add to a small pan and simmer. Meanwhile, whisk the egg yolks with the sugar in a medium bowl.

Pour half of the hot champagne cream over the yolks, whisking until combined.

Pour this mixture back into your pan and set over a low heat.

Cook while whisking continuously until the custard coats the back of a spoon.

Put the chopped chocolate in a heatproof bowl and strain the custard through a sieve over the chocolate. Leave for 45 seconds, then, beginning in the centre of the bowl, whisk until smooth. Pour the filling into your baked tart case and pop into the fridge to set for at least 4 hours or overnight.

TO SERVE

Dust the tart with cocoa powder and scatter over the dried rose petals.

Blend the tinned peaches until smooth.

Serve the peach purée with the tart, alongside fresh peaches and Chantilly cream.

Apply the advice you give to others to yourself. Never feel guilty for taking time out to look after your mental health: it is really, really important. Personally, I meditate every day, I do rapid tapping (a psycho-sensory therapy technique) and I have a dog, so I get outside in nature a lot. I also love cooking with my daughters, and I love having friends and family round to share a meal and this is really important to me.

KAREN HOWES (@KAREN_J_HOWES)

SHARE ALL YOUR PROBLEMS AND HOLD NOTHING IN.
A PROBLEM SHARED IS A PROBLEM HALVED.

DANNY O'DONOGHUE

BANANA ICE CREAM CHEESECAKE WITH BLUEBERRY COMPOTE

PREPARATION TIME: 30-45 MINUTES, PLUS CHILLING AND FREEZING | COOKING TIME: 15 MINUTES | SERVES 8-12

INGREDIENTS

FOR THE BASE

160g porridge oats

160g roasted whole hazelnuts

60ml coconut oil, plus extra for greasing the tin

185g golden syrup

Pinch of salt

FOR THE FILLING

7 bananas, chopped and frozen

2 tbsp golden syrup

1 tbsp cocoa powder

½ tsp ground cinnamon

FOR THE COMPOTE

250g fresh or frozen blueberries

½ lemon, zested and juiced

100g caster sugar

METHOD

FOR THE BASE

Grease the base and sides of a 20cm round loose-bottomed tin, 7.5cm deep.

Make the base of the cheesecake by toasting the oats and hazelnuts in a large frying pan on a medium heat for about 5 minutes until they just start to turn golden brown, making sure you stir all the time to keep the oats moving.

Pop them straight into a food processor and blitz to a fine crumb.

Now add the coconut oil, golden syrup and salt to the food processor and blitz again until it all clumps together.

Place the mixture into the prepared tin and, using the back of a spoon, press into the base and 2.5cm up the sides.

Leave the base to chill while you make the filling.

FOR THE FILLING

Take the chopped bananas out the freezer and put them into a food processor with the golden syrup, cocoa and cinnamon.

Leave for 5 minutes and allow the bananas to defrost just very slightly so that they process more easily, then blitz until you have what looks like a soft-scoop ice cream.

Quickly spoon the banana mixture on top of the chilled base and pop into the freezer.

FOR THE COMPOTE

Add the blueberries, lemon zest, lemon juice and caster sugar to a pan and stir over a medium heat until the blueberries have just softened.

Take the cheesecake out of the freezer and slide it out of the tin onto your serving dish.

Spoon the compote on top and leave for just a few minutes before slicing.

> Cooking, baking and being in the kitchen allows me to be creative in a focused way. When my mind feels all over the place, being in the kitchen helps me to put all of that aside and do one thing at a time. Walking also helps me to be present in the moment. Other ways of looking after my mental health include self-care – even something simple like running a bath and spending some quality time taking care of the physical body that houses me and gives me life – and prayer, as feeling close to God helps me to stay grounded, humble and grateful.
>
> NADIYA HUSSAIN (@NADIYAJHUSSAIN)

RASPBERRY &
ALMOND FLAPJACKS

PREPARATION TIME: 15-30 MINUTES | COOKING TIME: 30 MINUTES | SERVES 9

INGREDIENTS

125g unsalted butter, plus extra for greasing

75g dark brown sugar

50g caster sugar

50g golden syrup

1 tsp almond extract

Pinch of salt

250g rolled porridge oats

75g toasted flaked almonds

100g frozen raspberries

METHOD

Preheat your oven to 200°c/180°c fan/Gas Mark 6.

Grease and line a 20cm square cake tin with butter and parchment paper.

Put the butter, brown sugar, caster sugar, golden syrup, almond extract and salt into a pan over a medium heat and stir until they have all melted together.

Pour in the oats and 50g of the toasted flaked almonds, stirring until combined.

Pour the flapjack mixture into the prepared tin and press down with the back of a spoon to level the surface.

Sprinkle the frozen raspberries and remaining flaked almonds evenly over the top and press into the mixture.

Bake the flapjack in the preheated oven for 30 minutes until golden brown.

Leave in the tin to cool completely before removing and cutting into 9 squares (3 by 3).

"

I look after my mental health by making sure I give plenty of time to myself — working out, meditation, sleep — and having self-awareness about any triggers that cause me stress or anxiety.

ALEX CROCKFORD (@ALEXCROCKFORD)

ITALIAN INSPIRED SUMMER PUDDING

PREPARATION TIME: 25-40 MINUTES PLUS CHILLING OVERNIGHT | COOKING TIME: 5 MINUTES | SERVES 6

INGREDIENTS

200g raspberries

200g blackberries

200g strawberries, hulled and quartered

150g caster sugar

1 lemon, zested and juiced

175g sponge fingers

100g mascarpone

100g double cream

1 tbsp caster sugar

Extra fresh berries, to serve

Sprig of fresh mint (optional)

METHOD

Put all the berries, caster sugar, lemon zest and juice into a pan over a medium heat for 4-5 minutes, until the berries release their juices but still hold some of their shape.

Drain the mixture into a bowl so you reserve all the liquid.

Dip the sponge fingers into the warm berry juices on both sides and leave for 30 seconds until softened.

Snap them in half and place in the bottom of a 900ml pudding basin, working your way from the base up the sides, placing them horizontally so there are no gaps.

You can line your pudding basin with a strip of parchment paper going all the way across it to prevent it from sticking.

Once the basin is covered with soaked sponge fingers, fill it with your berry mixture.

Top with some more sponge fingers dipped into the berry juices, making sure that they're touching the sponge fingers on the inside of the basin to create a seal, pressing them together with your fingertips.

Drizzle with 2 or 3 tablespoons of the berry liquid if you have any left over.

Place a small plate on top of the bowl and top with two unopened tins to act as weights. Put the pudding into the fridge and leave it like this overnight.

When you're ready to serve, whip the mascarpone, double cream and caster sugar together for 4 minutes until you have soft peaks.

TO SERVE

Run a small knife around the inside of the pudding basin to loosen the sponge fingers.

Turn out the chilled pudding onto a large plate and serve with the whipped mascarpone cream, extra fresh berries and a sprig of mint on top.

> Don't be afraid to speak out. As I've got older, I have had more courage to talk about when I feel challenged, when I am mentally exhausted, when things are getting to me. Everyone has their challenges and we all try and cope in different ways. Try to be kind, even when others aren't, because you don't know what they might be going through.
>
> CAROLINE RUSH (@97CRUSH)

SOMETIMES THE EASY OPTION IS
TO RUN AWAY FROM OUR EMOTIONS,
BUT LEANING INTO THE PAIN ENABLES YOU
TO GROW STRONGER AND HEAL.

NIOMI SMART

FROM BEDER'S KITCHEN

From Beder's Kitchen is a charity cookbook containing a collection of recipes and reflections from amazing foodies around the world including head and executive chefs at some of the UK's leading restaurants; MasterChef winners; TV chefs; food bloggers; nutritionists; best-selling authors; a Great British Bake Off winner and mental health advocates.

Among those involved are Gordon Ramsay, world famous chef and TV personality; Yotam Ottolenghi, restaurateur, chef and best-selling author; Atul Kochhar, chef and TV regular; Carla Henriques, executive pastry chef at Hawksmoor; Michael Zee, author and creator of Symmetry Breakfast; Romy Gill, chef and TV regular; Judy Joo, host of Korean Food Made Simple; Joudie Kalla, author of Palestine on a Plate; Jack Blumenthal, chef and son of Heston; David Atherton, Great British Bake Off 2019 winner; Liz Earle, writer, TV presenter and author; and Miles Kirby, chef director at Caravan.

FOR MORE INFORMATION, PLEASE VISIT WWW.BEDER.ORG.UK/FROM-BEDERS-KITCHEN

FROM BEDER'S KITCHEN

RECIPES AND REFLECTIONS TO RAISE AWARENESS
AROUND MENTAL HEALTH AND SUICIDE PREVENTION
FROM FOODIES ALL OVER THE WORLD

STOCKISTS:

Harrods Waterstones WHOLE FOODS MARKET daylesford ORGANIC FARM GLOUCESTERSHIRE Virgin MEGASTORE

FEATURED IN:

The Telegraph theguardian WAITROSE & PARTNERS COUNTRY & TOWN HOUSE Good Housekeeping

BBC goodfood COUNTRY & TOWN INTERIORS VANITY FAIR HOTDINNERS euronews.

A

almond milk
Cacao, Peanut Butter & Banana Breakfast Smoothie 42
Creamy Carrot & Red Lentil Soup 52
Sweetcorn Ribs with Cashew Aioli Sauce 86
Creamy Cacao Mousse 188

almonds
Turmeric Fish Stew with Bulgur Wheat Salad 80
Raspberry & Almond Flapjacks 198

anchovies
Charred Chicken Pitas with Lemony Salsa Verde 96

apple cider vinegar
ACV Lemon Tonic 24
Turkey, Lemongrass & Ginger Meatballs 78

apples
Apple Crumble Pie 176

apricot
Honey & Sesame Muesli Bars 16
Turmeric Fish Stew with Bulgur Wheat Salad 80

asparagus
Spring Green Spaghetti 92

aubergine
Wild Rice, Roasted Aubergine & Sweet Potato Salad 68
Roasted Aubergine, Red Pepper & Prawn Pearl Barley 72
Aubergine Parmigiana 130

avocado
Homemade Sesame Bagels 44
Tuna Ceviche 124
Mexican Chicken & Lime Tortilla Soup 146

B

balsamic vinegar
Baked Cod with Spicy Butter Bean Stew & Olive Crumb 60
Aubergine Parmigiana 130

banana
Chocolate Chunk Banana Pancakes with Hazelnuts
& Maple Syrup 38
Cacao, Peanut Butter & Banana Breakfast Smoothie 42
Homemade Sesame Bagels 44
Banana Ice Cream Cheesecake with Blueberry Compote 196

beef
Vietnamese Style Sticky Shaking Beef 120
Sticky Korean Beef Ribs 132

black beans
Grilled Corn, Black Bean & Salsa Verde Tacos 56
Mixed Bean Burgers with Kimchi Relish 76
Crispy Tempeh Tacos 112

Mexican Chicken & Lime Tortilla Soup 146

blackberries
Italian Inspired Summer Pudding 200

blueberries
Banana Ice Cream Cheesecake with Blueberry Compote 196

broad beans
Spring Green Spaghetti 92

broccoli
Miso Hake Parcels 100
Broccoli Pesto Pasta 102

bulgur wheat
Turmeric Fish Stew with Bulgur Wheat Salad 80
Za'atar Chicken with Herby Bulgur Salad
& Harissa Yoghurt 114

butter beans
Baked Cod with Spicy Butter Bean Stew & Olive Crumb 60
Mixed Bean Burgers with Kimchi Relish 76
Turmeric Fish Stew with Bulgur Wheat Salad 80

buttermilk
Seeded Soda Bread 26
Southern Fried Chicken Burger 136

butternut squash
Butternut Squash Noodles with Satay Sauce
& Miso Mushrooms 64
Jamaican Oxtail Stew with Crispy Potatoes 160

C

cabbage
Turkey, Lemongrass & Ginger Meatballs 78
Salmon Poke Bowl 84
Charred Chicken Pitas with Lemony Salsa Verde 96

cacao
Cacao, Peanut Butter & Banana Breakfast Smoothie 42
Creamy Cacao Mousse 188

capers
Grilled Corn, Black Bean & Salsa Verde Tacos 56
Charred Chicken Pitas with Lemony Salsa Verde 96

caramel
Date & Salted Caramel Cake 174
Sticky Toffee Cheesecake Pudding 186

carrots
Creamy Carrot & Red Lentil Soup 52
Turkey, Lemongrass & Ginger Meatballs 78
Salmon Poke Bowl 84

cashew milk
Pear & Tahini Porridge 20

cashews
Sweetcorn Ribs with Cashew Aioli Sauce 86
Broccoli Pesto Pasta 102

Seafood Jambalaya 134

Jerk Chicken Skewers with Coconut Rice 144

Mexican Chicken & Lime Tortilla Soup 146

Pulled Pork Tostadas 168

linguine

Crab, Chilli & Lemon Pasta with Pangrattato 126

lobster

Lobster Mac 'n' Cheese 152

M

macaroni

Lobster Mac 'n' Cheese 152

mango chutney

One-Pan Tikka Roast Chicken 154

mango purée

Chicken, Kefir & Turmeric Curry 66

maple syrup

Pear & Tahini Porridge 20

Chocolate Chunk Banana Pancakes with
Hazelnuts & Maple Syrup 38

Butternut Squash Noodles with Satay Sauce
& Miso Mushrooms 64

marshmallows

Mexican Hot Chocolate Cake 190

mascarpone

Sticky Toffee Cheesecake Pudding 186

Italian Inspired Summer Pudding 200

mint sauce

Spiced Lamb Pizza 164

mirin

Sticky Korean Beef Ribs 132

miso paste

Creamy Carrot & Red Lentil Soup 52

Miso Mushroom Dumplings 58

Butternut Squash Noodles with Satay Sauce
& Miso Mushrooms 64

Mixed Bean Burgers with Kimchi Relish 76

Miso Hake Parcels 100

Crispy Tempeh Tacos 112

mixed peel

Barmbrack 180

mixed seeds

Honey & Sesame Muesli Bars 16

Seeded Soda Bread 26

monkfish

Turmeric Fish Stew with Bulgur Wheat Salad 80

mozzarella

Aubergine Parmigiana 130

Spiced Lamb Pizza 164

mushrooms

Miso Mushroom Dumplings 58

Butternut Squash Noodles with Satay Sauce
& Miso Mushrooms 64

Mixed Bean Burgers with Kimchi Relish 76

Crispy Tempeh Tacos 112

Chicken & Caramelised Leek Pie 150

mussels

Seafood Jambalaya 134

O

oats

Honey & Sesame Muesli Bars 16

Pear & Tahini Porridge 20

Oat Chocolate Chip Muffins 172

Apple Crumble Pie 176

Banana Ice Cream Cheesecake with Blueberry Compote 196

Raspberry & Almond Flapjacks 198

olives

Baked Cod with Spicy Butter Bean Stew & Olive Crumb 60

onion

Sumac Baked Feta with Crispy Chickpeas & Harissa Yoghurt 30

Crispy Potato Latkes with Sour Cream,
Smoked Salmon & Poached Eggs 36

Kedgeree 46

Creamy Carrot & Red Lentil Soup 52

Grilled Corn, Black Bean & Salsa Verde Tacos 56

Miso Mushroom Dumplings 58

Baked Cod with Spicy Butter Bean Stew & Olive Crumb 60

Chicken, Kefir & Turmeric Curry 66

Roasted Aubergine, Red Pepper & Prawn Pearl Barley 72

Creamy Salmon & New Potato Curry 74

Mixed Bean Burgers with Kimchi Relish 76

Turmeric Fish Stew with Bulgur Wheat Salad 80

Charred Chicken Pitas with Lemony Salsa Verde 96

Chicken Jalfrezi 104

Crispy Tempeh Tacos 112

Vietnamese Style Sticky Shaking Beef 120

Tuna Ceviche 124

Aubergine Parmigiana 130

Seafood Jambalaya 134

Taro with Pork 140

Keema with Peas & Roti 142

Jerk Chicken Skewers with Coconut Rice 144

Mexican Chicken & Lime Tortilla Soup 146

Lobster Mac 'n' Cheese 152

One-Pan Tikka Roast Chicken 154

Middle Eastern Slow-Cooked Lamb 156

Jamaican Oxtail Stew with Crispy Potatoes 160

Spiced Lamb Pizza 164

NOTES

This page is for your own notes about the recipes: ingredients you've swapped out, timings that work best for you and any additions that you or your family love... make them your own and have fun!

We hope you don't, but if you do come across any errors in the recipes, then you can let us know by emailing *inspire@beder.org.uk* and any updated recipes can be found at *www.beder.org.uk/eatwithbeder*

NOTES